The Writings of

Abraham Lincoln

Edited by
Arthur Brooks Lapsley

With an Introduction by
Theodore Roosevelt

Together with
The Essay on Lincoln, by Carl Schurz
The Address on Lincoln, by Joseph H. Choate
and The Life of Lincoln, by Noah Brooks

Volume Four
The Lincoln–Douglas Debates—II

G. P. Putnam's Sons
New York and London
The Knickerbocker Press
1905

Political Debates

between

Abraham Lincoln

and

Stephen A. Douglas

In the Senatorial Campaign of 1858 in Illinois;
including the preceding speeches of each
at Chicago, Springfield, etc.

Part II

CONTENTS

ILLUSTRATIONS

POLITICAL DEBATES

BETWEEN

LINCOLN AND DOUGLAS

FOURTH JOINT DEBATE, AT CHARLESTON,

September 18, 1858.

MR. LINCOLN'S SPEECH.

LADIES AND GENTLEMEN: It will be very difficult for an audience so large as this to hear distinctly what a speaker says, and consequently it is important that as profound silence be preserved as possible.

While I was at the hotel to-day, an elderly gentleman called upon me to know whether I was really in favor of producing a perfect equality between the negroes and white people. While I had not proposed to myself on this occasion to say much on that subject, yet as the question was asked me I thought I would occupy perhaps five minutes in saying something in regard to it. I will say, then, that I am not, nor ever have been, in favor of bringing about in any way the social and political equality of the white and black races; that I am not, nor ever have been, in favor of making voters or jurors of negroes, nor of qualifying them to hold office, nor to intermarry with white people; and I will say, in addition to this, that there is a physical difference between the white and black races which I believe will forever forbid the two races living together on terms of social and political equality. And inasmuch as they cannot so live, while they do remain together there, must be the position of superior and inferior, and I as much as any other man am in favor of having the superior position assigned to the white race. I say upon this occasion I do not perceive that because the white man is to have the superior position the negro should be denied everything. I do not understand that because I do not want a negro woman for a slave I must necessarily want her for a wife. My understanding is that I can just let her alone. I am now in my fiftieth year, and I certainly never have had a black woman for either a slave or a wife. So it seems to me quite possible for us to get along without making either slaves or wives of negroes. I will add to this that I have never seen, to my knowledge, a man, woman, or child who was in favor of producing a perfect equality, social and political, between negroes and white men. I recollect of but one distinguished instance that I ever heard of so frequently as to be entirely satisfied of its correctness, and that is the case of Judge Douglas's old friend Colonel Richard M. Johnson. I will also add to the remarks I have made (for I am not going to enter at large upon this subject), that I have never had the least apprehension that I or my friends would marry negroes if there was no law to keep them from it; but as Judge Douglas and his friends seem to be in great apprehension that they might, if there were no law to keep them from it, I give him the most solemn pledge that I will to the very last stand by the law of this State which forbids the marrying of white people with negroes. I will add one further word, which is this: that I do not understand that there is any place where an alteration of the social and political relations of the negro and the white man can be made, except in the State Legislature,—not in the Congress of the United States; and as I do not really apprehend the approach of any such thing myself, and as Judge Douglas seems to be in constant horror that some such danger is rapidly approaching, I propose as the best means to prevent it that the Judge be kept at home, and placed in the State Legislature to fight the measure. I do not propose dwelling longer at this time on this subject.

When Judge Trumbull, our other Senator in Congress, returned to Illinois in the month of August, he made a speech at Chicago, in which he made what may be called a *charge* against Judge Douglas, which I understand proved to be very offensive to him. The Judge was at that time out upon one of his speaking tours through the country, and when the news of it reached him, as I am informed, he denounced Judge Trumbull in rather harsh terms for having said what he did in regard to that matter. I was travelling at that time, and speaking at the same places with Judge Douglas on subsequent days, and when I heard of what Judge Trumbull had said of Douglas, and what Douglas had said back again, I felt that I was in a position where I could not remain entirely silent in regard to the matter.   Consequently, upon two or three occasions I alluded to it, and alluded to it in no other wise than to say that in regard to the charge brought by Trumbull against Douglas, I *personally* knew nothing, and sought to say nothing about it; that I did personally know Judge Trumbull; that I believed him to be a man of veracity; that I believed him to be a man of capacity sufficient to know very well whether an assertion he was making, as a conclusion drawn from a set of facts, was true or false; and as a conclusion of my own from that, I stated it as my belief if Trumbull should ever be called upon, he would prove everything he had said.   I said this upon two or three occasions.   Upon a subsequent occasion, Judge Trumbull spoke again before an audience at Alton, and upon that occasion not only repeated his charge against Douglas, but arrayed the evidence he relied upon to substantiate it.   This speech was published at length; and subsequently at Jacksonville Judge Douglas alluded to the matter.   In the course of his speech, and near the close of it, he stated in regard to myself what I will now read: "Judge Douglas proceeded to remark that he should not hereafter occupy his time in refuting such charges made by Trumbull, but that, Lincoln having indorsed the character of Trumbull for veracity, he should hold him (Lincoln) responsible for the slanders." I have done simply what I have told you, to subject me to this invitation to notice the charge. I now wish to say that it had not originally been my purpose to discuss that matter at all. But inasmuch as it seems to be the wish of Judge Douglas to hold me responsible for it, then for once in my life I will play General Jackson, and to the just extent I take the responsibility.

I wish to say at the beginning that I will hand to the reporters that portion of Judge Trumbull's Alton speech which was devoted to this matter, and also that portion of Judge Douglas's speech made at Jacksonville in answer to it. I shall thereby furnish the readers of this debate with the complete discussion between Trumbull and Douglas. I cannot now read them, for the reason that it would take half of my first hour to do so. I can only make some comments upon them. Trumbull's charge is in the following words: "Now, the charge is, that there was a plot entered into to have a constitution formed for Kansas, and put in force, without giving the people an opportunity to vote upon it, and that Mr. Douglas was in the plot." I will state, without quoting further, for all will have an opportunity of reading it hereafter, that Judge Trumbull brings forward what he regards as sufficient evidence to substantiate this charge.[1]

It will be perceived Judge Trumbull shows that Senator Bigler, upon the floor of the Senate, had declared there had been a conference among the senators, in which conference it was determined to have an enabling act passed for the people of Kansas to form a constitution under, and in this

[1] See Trumbull's speech at the close of this debate.

conference it was agreed among them that it was
best not to have a provision for submitting the constitution to a vote of the people after it should be
formed.   He then brings forward to show, and
showing, as he deemed, that Judge Douglas reported
the bill back to the Senate with that clause stricken
out.   He then shows that there was a new clause
inserted into the bill, which would in its nature
prevent a reference of the constitution back for a
vote of the people,—if, indeed, upon a mere silence
in the law, it could be assumed that they had the
right to vote upon it.   These are the general statements that he has made.

I propose to examine the points in Judge Douglas's
speech in which he attempts to answer that speech
of Judge Trumbull's.   When you come to examine
Judge Douglas's speech, you will find that the first
point he makes is: "Suppose it were true that there
was such a change in the bill, and that I struck it
out,—is that a proof of a plot to force a constitution
upon them against their will?"   His striking out
such a provision, if there was such a one in the bill,
he argues, does not establish the proof that it was
stricken out for the purpose of robbing the people of
that right.   I would say, in the first place, that that
would be a *most manifest* reason for it.   It is true, as
Judge Douglas states, that many Territorial bills
have passed without having such a provision in
them.   I believe it is true, though I am not certain,
that in some instances constitutions framed under
such bills have been submitted to a vote of the people
with the law silent upon the subject; but it does

not appear that they once had their enabling acts
framed with an express provision *for* submitting the
constitution to be framed to a vote of the people,
and then that they were stricken out when Congress
did not mean to alter the effect of the law. That
there have been bills which never had the provision
in, I do not question; but when was that provision
taken out of one that it was in? More especially
does this evidence tend to prove the proposition that
Trumbull advanced, when we remember that the
provision was stricken out of the bill almost simultaneously with the time that Bigler says there was
a conference among certain senators, and in which it
was agreed that a bill should be passed leaving that
out. Judge Douglas, in answering Trumbull, omits
to attend to the testimony of Bigler, that there was
a meeting in which it was agreed they should so frame
the bill that there should be no submission of the
constitution to a vote of the people. The Judge
does not notice this part of it. If you take this
as one piece of evidence, and then ascertain that
simultaneously Judge Douglas struck out a provision that did require it to be submitted, and put the
two together, I think it will make a pretty fair show
of proof that Judge Douglas did, as Trumbull says,
enter into a plot to put in force a constitution for
Kansas, without giving the people any opportunity
of voting upon it.

But I must hurry on. The next proposition that
Judge Douglas puts is this: "But upon examination
it turns out that the Toombs bill never did contain
a clause requiring the constitution to be submitted."

This is a mere question of fact, and can be determined by evidence. I only want to ask this question: Why did not Judge Douglas say that these
words were not stricken out of the Toombs bill, or
this bill from which it is alleged the provision was
stricken out,—a bill which goes by the name of
Toombs, because he originally brought it forward? I
ask why, if the Judge wanted to make a direct issue
with Trumbull, did he not take the exact proposition
Trumbull made in his speech, and say it was not
stricken out? Trumbull has given the exact words
that he says were in the Toombs bill, and he alleges
that when the bill came back, they were stricken
out. Judge Douglas does not say that the words
which Trumbull says were stricken out were not so
stricken out, but he says there was no provision in
the Toombs bill to submit the constitution to a vote
of the people. We see at once that he is merely
making an issue upon the meaning of the words.
He has not undertaken to say that Trumbull tells
a lie about these words being stricken out, but he
is really, when pushed up to it, only taking an issue
upon the meaning of the words. Now, then, if there
be any issue upon the meaning of the words, or if
there be upon the question of fact as to whether these
words were stricken out, I have before me what I
suppose to be a genuine copy of the Toombs bill, in
which it can be shown that the words Trumbull says
were in it were, in fact, originally there. If there be
any dispute upon the fact, I have got the documents
here to show they were there. If there be any controversy upon the sense of the words,—whether

these words which were stricken out really constituted a provision for submitting the matter to a
vote of the people,—as that is a matter of argument,
I think I may as well use Trumbull's own argument.
He says that the proposition is in these words:

"That the following propositions be and the same are
hereby offered to the said Convention of the people of
Kansas when formed, for their free acceptance or rejection; which, if accepted by the Convention *and ratified
by the people at the election for the adoption of the constitution*, shall be obligatory upon the United States and the
said State of Kansas."

Now, Trumbull alleges that these last words were
stricken out of the bill when it came back, and he
says this was a provision for submitting the constitution to a vote of the people; and his argument is
this: "Would it have been possible to ratify the
land propositions at the election for the adoption of
the constitution, unless such an election was to be
held?" This is Trumbull's argument. Now, Judge
Douglas does not meet the charge at all, but he
stands up and says there was no such proposition
in that bill for submitting the constitution to be
framed to a vote of the people. Trumbull admits
that the language is not a direct provision for submitting it, but it is a provision necessarily implied
from another provision. He asks you how it is possible to ratify the land proposition at the election for
the adoption of the constitution, if there was no
election to be held for the adoption of the constitution. And he goes on to show that it is not any less
a law because the provision is put in that indirect

shape than it would be if it were put directly.   But
I presume I have said enough to draw attention to
this point, and I pass it by also.

Another one of the points that Judge Douglas
makes upon Trumbull, and at very great length, is,
that Trumbull, while the bill was pending, said in a
speech in the Senate that he supposed the constitution to be made would have to be submitted to the
people.   He asks, if Trumbull thought so then, what
ground is there for anybody thinking otherwise now?
Fellow-citizens, this much may be said in reply:
That bill had been in the hands of a party to which
Trumbull did not belong.   It had been in the hands
of the committee at the head of which Judge
Douglas stood.   Trumbull perhaps had a printed
copy of the original Toombs bill.   I have not the
evidence on that point except a sort of inference I
draw from the general course of business there.
What alterations, or what provisions in the way of
altering, were going on in committee, Trumbull had
no means of knowing, until the altered bill was
reported back.   Soon afterwards, when it was reported back, there was a discussion over it, and perhaps Trumbull in reading it hastily in the altered
form did not perceive all the bearings of the alterations.   He was hastily borne into the debate, and
it does not follow that because there was something
in it Trumbull did not perceive, that something did
not exist.   More than this, is it true that what
Trumbull did can have any effect on what Douglas
did?   Suppose Trumbull had been in the plot with
these other men, would that let Douglas out of it?

Would it exonerate Douglas that Trumbull did n't then perceive he was in the plot? He also asks the question: Why did n't Trumbull propose to amend the bill, if he thought it needed any amendment? Why, I believe that everything Judge Trumbull had proposed, particularly in connection with this question of Kansas and Nebraska, since he had been on the floor of the Senate, had been promptly voted down by Judge Douglas and his friends. He had no promise that an amendment offered by him to anything on this subject would receive the slightest consideration. Judge Trumbull did bring to the notice of the Senate at that time the fact that there was no provision for submitting the constitution about to be made for the people of Kansas to a vote of the people. I believe I may venture to say that Judge Douglas made some reply to this speech of Judge Trumbull's, *but he never noticed that part of it at all.* And so the thing passed by. I think, then, the fact that Judge Trumbull offered no amendment does not throw much blame upon him; and if it did, it does not reach the question of fact *as to what Judge Douglas was doing.* I repeat, that if Trumbull had himself been in the plot, it would not at all relieve the others who were in it from blame. If I should be indicted for murder, and upon the trial it should be discovered that I had been implicated in that murder, but that the prosecuting witness was guilty too, that would not at all touch the question of my crime. It would be no relief to my neck that they discovered this other man who charged the crime upon me to be guilty too.

Another one of the points Judge Douglas makes upon Judge Trumbull is, that when he spoke in Chicago he made his charge to rest upon the fact that the bill had the provision in it for submitting the constitution to a vote of the people when it went into his (Judge Douglas's) hands, that it was missing when he reported it to the Senate, and that in a public speech he had subsequently said the alterations in the bill were made while it was in committee, and that they were made in consultation between him (Judge Douglas) and Toombs. And Judge Douglas goes on to comment upon the fact of Trumbull's adducing in his Alton speech the proposition that the bill not only came back with that proposition stricken out, but with another clause and another provision in it, saying that "until the complete execution of this Act there shall be no election in said Territory,"—which, Trumbull argued, was not only taking the provision for submitting to a vote of the people out of the bill, but was adding an affirmative one, in that it prevented the people from exercising the right under a bill that was merely silent on the question. Now, in regard to what he says, that Trumbull shifts the issue, that he shifts his ground,—and I believe he uses the term that, "it being proven false, he has changed ground,"— I call upon all of you, when you come to examine that portion of Trumbull's speech (for it will make a part of mine), to examine whether Trumbull has shifted his ground or not. I say he did not shift his ground, but that he brought forward his original charge and the evidence to sustain it yet more fully, but precisely as he originally made it. Then, in addition thereto, he brought in a new piece of evidence. He shifted no ground. He brought no new piece of evidence inconsistent with his former testimony; but he brought a new piece, tending, as he thought, and as I think, to prove his proposition. To illustrate: A man brings an accusation against another, and on trial the man making the charge introduces A and B to prove the accusation. At a second trial he introduces the same witnesses, who tell the same story as before, and a third witness, who tells the same thing, and in addition gives further testimony corroborative of the charge. So with Trumbull. There was no shifting of ground, nor inconsistency of testimony between the new piece of evidence and what he originally introduced.

But Judge Douglas says that he himself moved to strike out that last provision of the bill, and that on his motion it was stricken out and a substitute inserted. That I presume is the truth. I presume it is true that that last proposition was stricken out by Judge Douglas. Trumbull has not said it was not; Trumbull has himself said that it was so stricken out. He says: "I am now speaking of the bill as Judge Douglas reported it back. It was amended somewhat in the Senate before it passed, but I am speaking of it as he brought it back." Now, when Judge Douglas parades the fact that the provision was stricken out of the bill when it came back, he asserts nothing contrary to what Trumbull alleges. Trumbull has only said that he originally put it in,— not that he did not strike it out. Trumbull says it

was not in the bill when it went to the committee.
When it came back it was in, and Judge Douglas
said the alterations were made by him in consultation with Toombs. Trumbull alleges, therefore, as
his conclusion, that Judge Douglas put it in. Then,
if Douglas wants to contradict Trumbull and call him
a liar, let him say he did not put it in, and not that
he did n't take it out again. It is said that a bear
is sometimes hard enough pushed to drop a cub;
and so I presume it was in this case. I presume the
truth is that Douglas put it in, and afterward took
it out. That, I take it, is the truth about it. Judge
Trumbull says one thing, Douglas says another thing,
and the two don't contradict one another at all.
The question is, What did he put it in for? In the
first place, what did he take the other provision
out of the bill for,—the provision which Trumbull
argued was necessary for submitting the constitution
to a vote of the people? What did he take that out
for; and, having taken it out, what did he put this
in for? I say that in the run of things it is not
unlikely forces conspire to render it vastly expedient
for Judge Douglas to take that latter clause out again.
The question that Trumbull has made is that Judge
Douglas put it in; and he don't meet Trumbull at
all unless he denies that.

In the clause of Judge Douglas's speech upon this
subject he uses this language toward Judge Trumbull. He says: "He forges his evidence from
beginning to end; and by falsifying the record, he
endeavors to bolster up his false charge." Well,
that is a pretty serious statement — Trumbull

forges his evidence from beginning to end. Now,
upon my own authority I say that it is not true.
What is a forgery? Consider the evidence that
Trumbull has brought forward. When you come
to read the speech, as you will be able to, examine
whether the evidence is a forgery from beginning to
end. He had the bill or document in his hand like
that [holding up a paper]. He says that is a copy
of the Toombs bill,—the amendment offered by
Toombs. He says that is a copy of the bill as it was
introduced and went into Judge Douglas's hands.
Now, does Judge Douglas say that is a forgery?
That is one thing Trumbull brought forward.
Judge Douglas says he forged it from beginning to
end! That is the "beginning," we will say. Does
Douglas say that is a forgery? Let him say it to-day,
and we will have a subsequent examination upon
this subject. Trumbull then holds up another document like this, and says that is an exact copy of the
bill as it came back in the amended form out of
Judge Douglas's hands. Does Judge Douglas say
that is a forgery? Does he say it in his general
sweeping charge? Does he say so now? If he does
not, then take this Toombs bill and the bill in the
amended form, and it only needs to compare them
to see that the provision is in the one and not in the
other; it leaves the inference inevitable that it was
taken out.

But, while I am dealing with this question, let us
see what Trumbull's other evidence is. One other
piece of evidence I will read. Trumbull says there
are in this original Toombs bill these words:

"That the following propositions be and the same are hereby offered to the said Convention of the people of Kansas, when formed, for their free acceptance or rejection; which, if accepted by the Convention and ratified by the people at the election for the adoption of the constitution, shall be obligatory upon the United States and the said State of Kansas."

Now, if it is said that this is a forgery, we will open the paper here and see whether it is or not.   Again, Trumbull says, as he goes along, that Mr. Bigler made the following statement in his place in the Senate, December 9, 1857:

"I was present when that subject was discussed by senators before the bill was introduced, and the question was raised and discussed, whether the constitution, when formed, should be submitted to a vote of the people. It was held by those most intelligent on the subject that, in view of all the difficulties surrounding that Territory, the danger of any experiment at that time of a popular vote, it would be better there should be no such provision in the Toombs bill; and it was my understanding, in all the intercourse I had, that the Convention would make a constitution, and send it here, without submitting it to the popular vote."

Then Trumbull follows on:

"In speaking of this meeting again on the 21st December, 1857 [*Congressional Globe*, same vol., page 113], Senator Bigler said:
"'Nothing was further from my mind than to allude to any social or confidential interview. The meeting was not of that character. Indeed, it was semi-official,

and called to promote the public good. My recollection was clear that I left the conference under the impression that it had been deemed best to adopt measures to admit Kansas as a State through the agency of one popular election, and that for delegates to this Convention. This impression was stronger because I thought the spirit of the bill infringed upon the doctrine of non-intervention, to which I had great aversion; but with the hope of accomplishing a great good, and as no movement had been made in that direction in the Territory, I waived this objection, and concluded to support the measure. I have a few items of testimony as to the correctness of these impressions, and with their submission I shall be content. I have before me the bill reported by the senator from Illinois on the 7th of March, 1856, providing for the admission of Kansas as a State, the third section of which reads as follows:

" ' " That the following propositions be, and the same are hereby offered to the said Convention of the people of Kansas, when formed, for their free acceptance or rejection; which, if accepted by the Convention and ratified by the people at the election for the adoption of the constitution, shall be obligatory upon the United States and the said State of Kansas."

" 'The bill read in his place by the senator from Georgia on the 25th of June, and referred to the Committee on Territories, contained the same section word for word. Both these bills were under consideration at the conference referred to; but, sir, when the senator from Illinois reported the Toombs bill to the Senate with amendments, the next morning, it did not contain that portion of the third section which indicated to the Convention that the constitution should be approved by the people. The words "*and ratified by the people at the*

election for the adoption of the constitution " had been
stricken out.' "

Now, these things Trumbull says were stated by
Bigler upon the floor of the Senate on certain days,
and that they are recorded in the *Congressional Globe*
on certain pages.   Does Judge Douglas say this is a
forgery?   Does he say there is no such thing in the
Congressional Globe?   What does he mean when he
says Judge Trumbull forges his evidence from beginning to end?   So again he says in another place that
Judge Douglas, in his speech, December 9, 1857
(*Congressional Globe*, part I., page 15), stated:

"That during the last session of Congress, I [Mr.
Douglas] reported a bill from the Committee on Territories, to authorize the people of Kansas to assemble
and form a constitution for themselves.   Subsequently
the senator from Georgia [Mr. Toombs] brought forward
a substitute for my bill, which, *after having been modified
by him and myself in consultation*, was passed by the
Senate."

Now, Trumbull says this is a quotation from a
speech of Douglas, and is recorded in the *Congressional Globe.*   Is *it* a forgery?   Is it there or not?   It
may not be there, but I want the Judge to take these
pieces of evidence, and distinctly say they are
forgeries if he dare do it.

A voice: He will.

Mr. LINCOLN: Well, sir, you had better not commit
him.   He gives other quotations,—another from
Judge Douglas.   He says:

" I will ask the senator to show me an intimation, from

any one member of the Senate, in the whole debate on
the Toombs bill, and in the Union, from any quarter, that
the constitution was not to be submitted to the people.
I will venture to say that on all sides of the chamber it
was so understood at the time. If the opponents of the
bill had understood it was not, they would have made the
point on it; and if they had made it, we should certainly
have yielded to it, and put in the clause. That is a discovery made since the President found out that it was not
safe to take it for granted that that would be done, which
ought in fairness to have been done."

Judge Trumbull says Douglas made that speech,
and it is recorded. Does Judge Douglas say it is a
forgery, and was not true? Trumbull says somewhere, and I propose to skip it, but it will be found
by any one who will read this debate, that he did
distinctly bring it to the notice of those who were
engineering the bill, that it lacked that provision;
and then he goes on to give another quotation from
Judge Douglas, where Judge Trumbull uses this
language:

"Judge Douglas, however, on the same day and in the
same debate, probably recollecting or being reminded of
the fact that I had objected to the Toombs bill when
pending that it did not provide for a submission of the
constitution to the people, made another statement,
which is to be found in the same volume of the *Globe*,
page 22, in which he says:

"'That the bill was silent on this subject was true,
and my attention was called to that about the time it
was passed; and I took the fair construction to be, that
powers not delegated were reserved, and that of course
the constitution would be submitted to the people.'

"Whether this statement is consistent with the statement just before made, that had the point been made it would have been yielded to, or that it was a new discovery, you will determine."

So I say. I do not know whether Judge Douglas will dispute this, and yet maintain his position that Trumbull's evidence "was forged from beginning to end." I will remark that I have not got these *Congressional Globes* with me. They are large books, and difficult to carry about, and if Judge Douglas shall say that on these points where Trumbull has quoted from them there are no such passages there, I shall not be able to prove they are there upon this occasion, but I will have another chance. Whenever he points out the forgery and says, "I declare that this particular thing which Trumbull has uttered is not to be found where he says it is," then my attention will be drawn to that, and I will arm myself for the contest,—stating now that I have not the slightest doubt on earth that I will find every quotation just where Trumbull says it is. Then the question is, How can Douglas call that a forgery? How can he make out that it is a forgery? What is a forgery? It is the bringing forward something in writing or in print purporting to be of certain effect when it is altogether untrue. If you come forward with my note for one hundred dollars when I have never given such a note, there is a forgery. If you come forward with a letter purporting to be written by me which I never wrote, there is another forgery. If you produce anything in writing or in print saying it is so and so, the document not being genuine, a

forgery has been committed. How do you make this
a forgery when every piece of the evidence is genuine?
If Judge Douglas does say these documents and
quotations are false and forged, he has a full right
to do so; but until he does it specifically, we don't
know how to get at him. If he does say they are
false and forged, I will then look further into it, and
I presume I can procure the certificates of the proper
officers that they are genuine copies. I have no
doubt each of these extracts will be found exactly
where Trumbull says it is. Then I leave it to you if
Judge Douglas, in making his sweeping charge that
Judge Trumbull's evidence is forged from beginning
to end, at all meets the case,—if that is the way to
get at the facts. I repeat again, if he will point out
which one is a forgery, I will carefully examine it,
and if it proves that any one of them is really a
forgery, it will not be me who will hold to it any
longer. I have always wanted to deal with everyone
I meet candidly and honestly. If I have made any
assertion not warranted by facts, and it is pointed
out to me, I will withdraw it cheerfully. But I do
not choose to see Judge Trumbull calumniated, and
the evidence he has brought forward branded in
general terms "a forgery from beginning to end."
This is not the legal way of meeting a charge, and I
submit to all intelligent persons, both friends of
Judge Douglas and of myself, whether it is.

The point upon Judge Douglas is this: The bill
that went into his hands had the provision in it for a
submission of the constitution to the people; and I
say its language amounts to an express provision for

a submission, and that he took the provision out.
He says it was known that the bill was silent in this
particular; *but I say, Judge Douglas, it was not silent
when you got it.* It was vocal with the declaration,
when you got it, for a submission of the constitution
to the people. And now, my direct question to
Judge Douglas is, to answer why, if he deemed the
bill silent on this point, he found it necessary to
strike out those particular harmless words. If he
had found the bill silent and without this provision,
he might say what he does now. If he supposes it
was implied that the constitution would be submitted to a vote of the people, how could these two
lines so encumber the statute as to make it necessary
to strike them out? How could he infer that a
submission was still implied, after its express provision had been stricken from the bill? I find the
bill vocal with the provision, while he silenced it.
He took it out, and although he took out the other
provision preventing a submission to a vote of the
people, I ask, *Why did you first put it in?* I ask him
whether he took the original provision out, which
Trumbull alleges was in the bill. If he admits that he
did take it, *I ask him what he did it for.* It looks to us
as if he had altered the bill. If it looks differently to
him,—if he has a different reason for his action from
the one we assign him—he can tell it. I insist upon
knowing why he made the bill silent upon that point
when it was vocal before he put his hands upon it.

I was told, before my last paragraph, that my
time was within three minutes of being out. I presume it is expired now; I therefore close.

LADIES AND GENTLEMEN: I had supposed that we
assembled here to-day for the purpose of a joint discussion between Mr. Lincoln and myself upon the
political questions that now agitate the whole country. The rule of such discussions is, that the opening speaker shall touch upon all the points he
intends to discuss, in order that his opponent, in
reply, shall have the opportunity of answering them.
Let me ask you what questions of public policy,
relating to the welfare of this State or the Union,
has Mr. Lincoln discussed before you? Mr. Lincoln
simply contented himself at the outset by saying that
he was not in favor of social and political equality
between the white man and the negro, and did not
desire the law so changed as to make the latter
voters or eligible to office. I am glad that I have
at last succeeded in getting an answer out of him
upon this question of negro citizenship and eligi-
bility to office, for I have been trying to bring
him to the point on it ever since this canvass
commenced.

I will now call your attention to the question
which Mr. Lincoln has occupied his entire.time in
discussing. He spent his whole hour in retailing
a charge made by Senator Trumbull against me.
The circumstances out of which that charge was
manufactured occurred prior to the last Presidential
election, over two years ago. If the charge was true,
why did not Trumbull make it in 1856, when I was
discussing the questions of that day all over this

State with Lincoln and him, and when it was perti-
nent to the then issue? He was then as silent as the
grave on the subject. If that charge was true, the
time to have brought it forward was the canvass
of 1856, the year when the Toombs bill passed the
Senate. When the facts were fresh in the public
mind, when the Kansas question was the paramount
question of the day, and when such a charge would
have had a material bearing on the election, why
did he and Lincoln remain silent then, knowing that
such a charge could be made and proven if true?
Were they not false to you and false to the country in
going through that entire campaign concealing their
knowledge of this enormous conspiracy which, Mr.
Trumbull says, he then knew and would not tell?
Mr. Lincoln intimates, in his speech, a good reason
why Mr. Trumbull would not tell, for he says that it
might be true, as I proved that it was at Jacksonville,
that Trumbull was also in the plot, yet that the fact
of Trumbull's being in the plot would not in any way
relieve me. He illustrates this argument by sup-
posing himself on trial for murder, and says that it
would be no extenuating circumstance if, on his trial
another man was found to be a party to his crime.
Well, if Trumbull was in the plot, and concealed
it in order to escape the odium which would have
fallen upon himself, I ask you whether you can
believe him now when he turns State's evidence, and
avows his own infamy in order to implicate me. I
am amazed that Mr. Lincoln should now come forward and indorse that charge, occupying his whole
hour in reading Mr. Trumbull's speech in support of

it. Why, I ask, does not Mr. Lincoln make a speech of his own instead of taking up his time reading Trumbull's speech at Alton? I supposed that Mr. Lincoln was capable of making a public speech on his own account, or I should not have accepted the banter from him for a joint discussion. ["How about the charges?"] Do not trouble yourselves. I am going to make my speech in my own way, and I trust, as the Democrats listened patiently and respectfully to Mr. Lincoln, that his friends will not interrupt me when I am answering him. When Mr. Trumbull returned from the East, the first thing he did when he landed in Chicago was to make a speech wholly devoted to assaults upon my public character and public action. Up to that time I had never alluded to his course in Congress, or to him directly or indirectly, and hence his assaults upon me were entirely without provocation and without excuse. Since then he has been travelling from one end of the State to the other, repeating his vile charge. I propose now to read it in his own language:

"Now, fellow-citizens, I make the distinct charge that there was a preconcerted arrangement and plot entered into by the very men who now claim credit for opposing a constitution formed and put in force without giving the people any opportunity to pass upon it. This, my friends, is a serious charge, but I charge it to-night that the very men who traverse the country under banners proclaiming popular sovereignty, by design concocted a bill on purpose to force a constitution upon that people."

In answer to some one in the crowd who asked him a question, Trumbull said:

"And you want to satisfy yourself that he was in the plot to force a constitution upon that people? I will satisfy you. I will cram the truth down any honest man's throat until he cannot deny it. And to the man who does deny it, I will cram the lie down his throat till he shall cry 'Enough!'

"It is preposterous; it is the most damnable effrontery that man ever put on, to conceal a scheme to defraud and cheat the people out of their rights, and then claim credit for it."

That is the polite language Senator Trumbull applied to me, his colleague, when I was two hundred miles off. Why did he not speak out as boldly in the Senate of the United States, and cram the lie down my throat when I denied the charge, first made by Bigler, and made him take it back? You all recollect how Bigler assaulted me when I was engaged in a hand-to-hand fight, resisting a scheme to force a constitution on the people of Kansas against their will. He then attacked me with this charge; but I proved its utter falsity, nailed the slander to the counter, and made him take the back track. There is not an honest man in America who read that debate who will pretend that the charge is true. Trumbull was then present in the Senate, face to face with me; and why did he not then rise and repeat the charge, and say he would cram the lie down my throat? I tell you that Trumbull then knew it was a lie. He knew that Toombs denied that there ever was a clause in the bill he brought forward calling for and requiring a submission of the Kansas Constitution to the people. I will tell you what the facts of the case were: I introduced a bill to authorize the people of Kansas to form a constitution, and come into the Union as a State whenever they should have the requisite population for a member of Congress, and Mr. Toombs proposed a substitute, authorizing the people of Kansas, with their then population of only 25,000, to form a constitution, and come in at once. The question at issue was, whether we would admit Kansas with a population of 25,000 or make her wait until she had the ratio entitling her to a representative in Congress, which was 93,420. That was the point of dispute in the Committee on Territories, to which both my bill and Mr. Toombs's substitute had been referred. I was overruled by a majority of the committee, my proposition rejected, and Mr. Toombs's proposition to admit Kansas then, with her population of 25,000, adopted. Accordingly a bill to carry out his idea of immediate admission was reported as a substitute for mine; the only points at issue being, as I have already said, the question of population, and the adoption of safeguards against frauds at the election. Trumbull knew this,—the whole Senate knew it,—and hence he was silent at that time. He waited until I became engaged in this canvass, and finding that I was showing up Lincoln's Abolitionism and negro equality doctrines, that I was driving Lincoln to the wall, and white men would not support his rank Abolitionism, he came back from the East and trumped up a system of charges against me, hoping that I would be compelled to occupy my entire time in defending myself, so that I would not be able to show up the enormity of the principles of the Abolitionists. Now, the only reason, and the true reason, why Mr. Lincoln has occupied the whole of his first hour in this issue between Trumbull and myself, is, to conceal from this vast audience the real questions which divide the two great parties.

I am not going to allow them to waste much of my time with these personal matters. I have lived in this State twenty-five years, most of that time have been in public life, and my record is open to you all. If that record is not enough to vindicate me from these petty, malicious assaults, I despise ever to be elected to office by slandering my opponents and traducing other men. Mr. Lincoln asks you to elect him to the United States Senate to-day solely because he and Trumbull can slander me. Has he given any other reason? Has he avowed what he was desirous to do in Congress on any one question? He desires to ride into office not upon his own merits, not upon the merits and soundness of his principles, but upon his success in fastening a stale old slander upon me.

I wish you to bear in mind that up to the time of the introduction of the Toombs bill, and after its introduction, there had never been an Act of Congress for the admission of a new State which contained a clause requiring its constitution to be submitted to the people. The general rule made the law silent on the subject, taking it for granted that the people would demand and compel a popular vote on the ratification of their constitution. Such was the general rule under Washington, Jefferson, Madison, Jackson, and Polk, under the Whig Presidents and the Democratic Presidents, from the beginning of the government down, and nobody dreamed that an effort would ever be made to abuse the power thus confided to the people of a Territory. For this reason our attention was not called to the fact of whether there was or was not a clause in the Toombs bill compelling submission, but it was taken for granted that the constitution would be submitted to the people whether the law compelled it or not.

Now, I will read from the report by me as chairman of the Committee on Territories at the time I reported back the Toombs substitute to the Senate. It contained several things which I had voted against in committee, but had been overruled by a majority of the members, and it was my duty as chairman of the Committee to report the bill back as it was agreed upon by them. The main point upon which I had been overruled was the question of population. In my report accompanying the Toombs bill, I said:

"In the opinion of your Committee, whenever a constitution shall be formed in any Territory, preparatory to its admission into the Union as a State, justice, the genius of our institutions, the whole theory of our republican system, imperatively demand that the voice of the people shall be fairly expressed, and their will embodied in that fundamental law, without fraud, or violence, or intimidation, or any other improper or unlawful influence, and subject to no other restrictions than those imposed by the Constitution of the United States."

There you find that we took it for granted that the constitution was to be submitted to the people, whether the bill was silent on the subject or not. Suppose I had reported it so, following the example of Washington, Adams, Jefferson, Madison, Monroe, Adams, Jackson, Van Buren, Harrison, Tyler, Polk, Taylor, Fillmore, and Pierce, would that fact have been evidence of a conspiracy to force a constitution upon the whole people of Kansas against their will? If the charge which Mr. Lincoln makes be true against me, it is true against Zachary Taylor, Millard Fillmore, and every Whig President, as well as every Democratic President, and against Henry Clay, who, in the Senate or House, for forty years advocated bills similar to the one I reported, no one of them containing a clause compelling the submission of the constitution to the people. Are Mr. Lincoln and Mr. Trumbull prepared to charge upon all those eminent men, from the beginning of the government down to the present day, that the absence of a provision compelling submission, in the various bills passed by them, authorizing the people of Territories to form State constitutions, is evidence of a corrupt design on their part to force a constitution upon an unwilling people?

I ask you to reflect on these things, for I tell you that there is a conspiracy to carry this election for the Black Republicans by slander, and not by fair means. Mr. Lincoln's speech this day is conclusive evidence of the fact. He has devoted his entire time to an issue between Mr. Trumbull and myself, and has not uttered a word about the

politics of the day. Are you going to elect Mr.
Trumbull's colleague upon an issue between Mr.
Trumbull and me? I thought I was running against
Abraham Lincoln, that he claimed to be my opponent, had challenged me to a discussion of the
public questions of the day with him, and was discussing these questions with me; but it turns out
that his only hope is to ride into office on Trumbull's back, who will carry him by falsehood.

Permit me to pursue this subject a little further.
An examination of the record proves that Trumbull's
charge—that the Toombs bill originally contained
a clause requiring the constitution to be submitted
to the people—*is false*. The printed copy of the bill
which Mr. Lincoln held up before you, and which he
pretends contains such a clause, merely contains a
clause requiring a submission of the land grant, and
*there is no clause in it requiring a submission of the
constitution*. Mr. Lincoln cannot find such a clause
in it. My report shows that we took it for granted
that the people would require a submission of the
constitution, and secure it for themselves. There
never was a clause in the Toombs bill requiring the
constitution to be submitted; Trumbull knew it at
the time, and his speech made on the night of its
passage discloses the fact that he knew it was silent
on the subject. Lincoln pretends, and tells you,
that Trumbull has not changed his evidence in support of his charge since he made his speech in
Chicago. Let us see. The Chicago *Times* took up
Trumbull's Chicago speech, compared it with the
official records of Congress, and proved that speech

to be false in its charge that the original Toombs bill required a submission of the constitution to the people. Trumbull then saw that he was caught, and his falsehood exposed, and he went to Alton, and, under the very walls of the penitentiary, made a new speech, in which he predicated his assault upon me in the allegation that I had caused to be voted into the Toombs bill a clause which prohibited the Convention from submitting the constitution to the people, and quoted what he pretended was the clause. Now, has not Mr. Trumbull entirely changed the evidence on which he bases his charge? The clause which he quoted in his Alton speech (which he has published and circulated broadcast over the State) as having been put into the Toombs bill by me, is in the following words: "And until the complete execution of this Act, no other election shall be held in said Territory."

Trumbull says that the object of that amendment was to prevent the Convention from submitting the constitution to a vote of the people.

Now, I will show you that when Trumbull made that statement at Alton he knew it to be untrue. I read from Trumbull's speech in the Senate on the Toombs bill on the night of its passage. He then said:

"There is nothing said in this bill, so far as I have discovered, about submitting the constitution, which is to be formed, to the people for their sanction or rejection. Perhaps the Convention will have the right to submit it, if it should think proper, but it is certainly not compelled to do so, according to the provisions of the bill."

Thus you see that Trumbull, when the bill was on its passage in the Senate, said that it was silent on the subject of submission, and that there was nothing in the bill one way or the other on it. In his Alton speech he says there was a clause in the bill preventing its submission to the people, and that I had it voted in as an amendment. Thus I convict him of falsehood and slander by quoting from him, on the passage of the Toombs bill in the Senate of the United States, his own speech, made on the night of July 2, 1856, and reported in the *Congressional Globe* for the first session of the thirty-fourth Congress, vol. 33. What will you think of a man who makes a false charge, and falsifies the records to prove it? I will now show you that the clause which Trumbull says was put in the bill on my motion was never put in at all by me, but was stricken out on my motion, and another substituted in its place. I call your attention to the same volume of the *Congressional Globe* to which I have already referred, page 795, where you will find the following report of the proceedings of the Senate:

"Mr. DOUGLAS: I have an amendment to offer from the Committee on Territories. On page 8, section 11, strike out the words 'until the complete execution of this Act, no other election shall be held in said Territory,' and insert the amendment which I hold in my hand."

You see from this that I moved to strike out the very words that Trumbull says I put in. The Committee on Territories overruled me in committee, and put the clause in; but as soon as I got the bill back

3

into the Senate, I moved to strike it out, and put
another clause in its place. On the same page you
will find that my amendment was agreed to *unanimously*. I then offered another amendment, recognizing the right of the people of Kansas, under the
Toombs bill, to order just such elections as they saw
proper. You can find it on page 796 of the same
volume. I will read it:

"Mr. DOUGLAS: I have another amendment to offer
from the Committee, to follow the amendment which has
been adopted. The bill reads now: 'And until the complete execution of this Act, no other election shall be
held in said Territory.' It has been suggested that it
should be modified in this way, 'And to avoid conflict
in the complete execution of this Act, all other elections
in said Territory are hereby postponed until such time
as said Convention shall appoint,' so that they can appoint the day in the event that there should be a failure
to come into the Union."

The amendment was *unanimously* agreed to,—
clearly and distinctly recognizing the right of the
convention to order just as many elections as they
saw proper in the execution of the act. Trumbull
concealed in his Alton speech the fact that the clause
he quoted had been stricken out in my motion, and
the other fact that this other clause was put in the
bill on my motion, and made the false charge that I
incorporated into the bill a clause preventing submission, in the face of the fact, that, on my motion, the bill was so amended before it passed as to
recognize in express words the right and duty of
submission.

On this record that I have produced before you, I repeat my charge that Trumbull did falsify the public records of the country, in order to make his charge against me, and I tell Mr. Abraham Lincoln that if he will examine these records, he will then know that what I state is true. Mr. Lincoln has this day indorsed Mr. Trumbull's veracity after he had my word for it that that veracity was proved to be violated and forfeited by the public records. It will not do for Mr. Lincoln, in parading his calumnies against me, to put Mr. Trumbull between him and the odium and responsibility which justly attaches to such calumnies. I tell him that I am as ready to prosecute the indorser as the maker of a forged note. I regret the necessity of occupying my time with these petty personal matters. It is unbecoming the dignity of a canvass for an office of the character for which we are candidates. When I commenced the canvass at Chicago, I spoke of Mr. Lincoln in terms of kindness as an old friend; I said that he was a good citizen, of unblemished character, against whom I had nothing to say. I repeated these complimentary remarks about him in my successive speeches, until he became the indorser for these and other slanders against me. If there is anything personally disagreeable, uncourteous, or disreputable in these personalities, the sole responsibility rests on Mr. Lincoln, Mr. Trumbull, and their backers.

I will show you another charge made by Mr. Lincoln against me, as an offset to his declaration of willingness to take back anything that is incorrect, and to correct any false statement he may have made. He has several times charged that the Supreme Court, President Pierce, President Buchanan, and myself, at the time I introduced the Nebraska Bill in January, 1854, at Washington, entered into a conspiracy to establish slavery all over this country. I branded this charge as a falsehood, and then he repeated it, asked me to analyze its truth and answer it. I told him: "Mr. Lincoln, I know what you are after—you want to occupy my time in personal matters, to prevent me from showing up the revolutionary principles which the Abolition party—whose candidate you are—have proclaimed to the world." But he asked me to analyze his proof, and I did so. I called his attention to the fact that at the time the Nebraska Bill was introduced, there was no such case as the Dred Scott case pending in the Supreme Court, nor was it brought there for years afterwards, and hence that it was impossible there could have been any conspiracy between the judges of the Supreme Court and the other parties involved. I proved by the record that the charge was false, and what did he answer? Did he take it back like an honest man and say that he had been mistaken? No; he repeated the charge, and said that, although there was no such case pending that year, there was an understanding between the Democratic owners of Dred Scott and the judges of the Supreme Court and other parties involved, that the case should be brought up. I then demanded to know who these Democratic owners of Dred Scott were. He could not or would not tell; he did not know. In truth, there were no

Democratic owners of Dred Scott on the face of the
land. Dred Scott was owned at that time by the
Rev. Dr. Chaffee, an Abolition member of Congress
from Springfield, Massachusetts, and his wife; and
Mr. Lincoln ought to have known that Dred Scott
was so owned, for the reason that as soon as the
decision was announced by the court Dr. Chaffee
and his wife executed a deed emancipating him, and
put that deed on record. It was a matter of public
record, therefore, that at the time the case was taken
to the Supreme Court Dred Scott was owned by an
Abolition member of Congress, a friend of Lincoln's
and a leading man of his party, while the defence was
conducted by Abolition lawyers,—and thus the Abolitionists managed both sides of the case. I have exposed these facts to Mr. Lincoln, and yet he will not
withdraw his charge of conspiracy. I now submit
to you whether you can place any confidence in a
man who continues to make a charge when its utter
falsity is proven by the public records. I will state
another fact to show how utterly reckless and un-
scrupulous this charge against the Supreme Court,
President Pierce, President Buchanan, and myself is.
Lincoln says that President Buchanan was in the
conspiracy at Washington in the winter of 1854,
when the Nebraska Bill was introduced. The history
of this country shows that James Buchanan was at
that time representing this country at the Court of
St. James, Great Britain, with distinguished ability
and usefulness, that he had not been in the United
States for nearly a year previous, and that he did
not return until about three years after. Yet Mr.

Lincoln keeps repeating this charge of conspiracy against Mr. Buchanan when the public records prove it to be untrue. Having proved it to be false as far as the Supreme Court and President Buchanan are concerned, I drop it, leaving the public to say whether I, by myself, without their concurrence, could have gone into a conspiracy with them. My friends, you see that the object clearly is to conduct the canvass on personal matters, and hunt me down with charges that are proven to be false by the public records of the country. I am willing to throw open my whole public and private life to the inspection of any man or all men who desire to investigate it. Having resided among you twenty-five years, during nearly the whole of which time a public man, exposed to more assaults, perhaps more abuse, than any man living of my age, or who ever did live, and having survived it all and still commanded your confidence, I am willing to trust to your knowledge of me and my public conduct without making any more defence against these assaults.

Fellow-citizens, I came here for the purpose of discussing the leading political topics which now agitate the country. I have no charges to make against Mr. Lincoln, none against Mr. Trumbull, and none against any man who is a candidate, except in repelling their assaults upon me. If Mr. Lincoln is a man of bad character, I leave you to find it out; if his votes in the past are not satisfactory, I leave others to ascertain the fact; if his course on the Mexican war was not in accordance with your notions of patriotism and fidelity to our own country as against a public enemy, I leave you to ascertain the fact. I have no assaults to make upon him, except to trace his course on the questions that now divide the country and engross so much of the people's attention.

You know that prior to 1854 this country was divided into two great political parties, one the Whig, the other the Democratic. I, as a Democrat for twenty years prior to that time, had been in public discussions in this State as an advocate of Democratic principles, and I can appeal with confidence to every old-line Whig within the hearing of my voice to bear testimony that during all that period I fought you Whigs like a man on every question that separated the two parties. I had the highest respect for Henry Clay as a gallant party leader, as an eminent statesman, and as one of the bright ornaments of this country; but I conscientiously believed that the Democratic party was right on the questions which separated the Democrats from the Whigs. The man does not live who can say that I ever personally assailed Henry Clay or Daniel Webster, or any one of the leaders of that great party, whilst I combated with all my energy the measures they advocated. What did we differ about in those days? Did Whigs and Democrats differ about this slavery question? On the contrary, did we not, in 1850, unite to a man in favor of that system of Compromise measures which Mr. Clay introduced, Webster defended, Cass supported, and Fillmore approved and made the law of the land by his signature? While we agreed on those Compromise measures, we

differed about a bank, the tariff, distribution, the
specie circular, the sub-treasury, and other questions
of that description.   Now, let me ask you which one
of those questions on which Whigs and Democrats
then differed now remains to divide the two great
parties?   Every one of those questions which divided
Whigs and Democrats has passed away, the country
has outgrown them, they have passed into history.
Hence it is immaterial whether you were right or I
was right on the bank, the sub-treasury, and other
questions, because they no longer continue living
issues.   What, then, has taken the place of those
questions about which we once differed?   The
slavery question has now become the leading and
controlling issue; that question on which you and I
agreed, on which the Whigs and Democrats united,
has now become the leading issue between the
national Democracy on the one side and the Republican, or Abolition, party on the other.

Just recollect for a moment the memorable contest
of 1850, when this country was agitated from its
centre to its circumference by the slavery agitation.
All eyes in this nation were then turned to the three
great lights that survived the days of the Revolution.
They looked to Clay, then in retirement at Ashland,
and to Webster and Cass, in the United States Senate.
Clay had retired to Ashland, having, as he supposed,
performed his mission on earth, and was preparing
himself for a better sphere of existence in another
world.   In that retirement he heard the discordant,
harsh, and grating sounds of sectional strife and disunion, and he aroused and came forth and resumed

his seat in the Senate, that great theatre of his great deeds. From the moment that Clay arrived among us he became the leader of all the Union men, whether Whigs or Democrats. For nine months we each assembled, each day, in the council-chamber, Clay in the chair, with Cass upon his right hand, and Webster upon his left, and the Democrats and Whigs gathered around, forgetting differences, and only animated by one common, patriotic sentiment, to devise means and measures by which we could defeat the mad and revolutionary scheme of the Northern Abolitionists and Southern Disunionists. We did devise those means, Clay brought them forward, Cass advocated them, the Union Democrats and Union Whigs voted for them, Fillmore signed them, and they gave peace and quiet to the country. Those Compromise measures of 1850 were founded upon the great fundamental principle that the people of each State and each Territory ought to be left free to form and regulate their own domestic institutions in their own way, subject only to the Federal Constitution. I will ask every old-line Democrat and every old-line Whig within the hearing of my voice if I have not truly stated the issues as they then presented themselves to the country. You recollect that the Abolitionists raised a howl of indignation, and cried for vengeance and the destruction of Democrats and Whigs both, who supported those Compromise measures of 1850. When I returned home to Chicago, I found the citizens inflamed and infuriated against the authors of those great measures. Being the only man in that city who was held

responsible for affirmative votes on all those measures,
I came forward and addressed the assembled inhabitants, defended each and every one of Clay's Compromise measures as they passed the Senate and the
House and were approved by President Fillmore.
Previous to that time, the city council had passed
resolutions nullifying the Act of Congress, and in-
structing the police to withhold all assistance from
its execution; but the people of Chicago listened to
my defence, and, like candid, frank, conscientious
men, when they became convinced that they had
done an injustice to Clay, Webster, Cass, and all of us
who had supported those measures, they repealed
their nullifying resolutions, and declared that the
laws should be executed and the supremacy of the
Constitution maintained.   Let it always be recorded
in history to the immortal honor of the people of Chicago that they returned to their duty when they
found that they were wrong, and did justice to those
whom they had blamed and abused unjustly.
When the Legislature of this State assembled that
year, they proceeded to pass resolutions approving
the Compromise measures of 1850.   When the Whig
party assembled in 1852 at Baltimore in National
Convention for the last time, to nominate Scott for
the presidency, they adopted as a part of their platform the Compromise measures of 1850, as the cardinal plank upon which every Whig would stand,
and by which he would regulate his future conduct.
When the Democratic party assembled at the same
place one month after, to nominate General Pierce,
we adopted the same platform so far as those Com-

promise measures were concerned, agreeing that we would stand by those glorious measures as a cardinal article in the Democratic faith. Thus you see that in 1852 all the old Whigs and all the old Democrats stood on a common plank so far as this slavery question was concerned, differing on other questions.

Now, let me ask, how is it that since that time so many of you Whigs have wandered from the true path marked out by Clay, and carried out broad and wide by the great Webster? How is it that so many old-line Democrats have abandoned the old faith of their party, and joined with Abolitionism and Free-soilism to overturn the platform of the old Democrats, and the platform of the old Whigs? You cannot deny that since 1854 there has been a great revolution on this one question. How has it been brought about? I answer, that no sooner was the sod grown green over the grave of the immortal Clay, no sooner was the rose planted on the tomb of the godlike Webster, than many of the leaders of the Whig party, such as Seward of New York, and his followers, led off and attempted to Abolitionize the Whig party, and transfer all your old Whigs, bound hand and foot, into the Abolition camp. Seizing hold of the temporary excitement produced in this country by the introduction of the Nebraska Bill, the disappointed politicians in the Democratic party united with the disappointed politicians in the Whig party, and endeavored to form a new party, composed of all the Abolitionists, of Abolitionized Democrats and Abolitionized Whigs, banded together in an Abolition platform.

And who led that crusade against national principles in this State? I answer, Abraham Lincoln on behalf of the Whigs, and Lyman Trumbull on behalf of the Democrats, formed a scheme by which they would Abolitionize the two great parties in this State, on condition that Lincoln should be sent to the United States Senate in place of General Shields, and that Trumbull should go to Congress from the Belleville District until I would be accommodating enough either to die or resign for his benefit, and then he was to go to the Senate in my place. You all remember that during the year 1854 these two worthy gentlemen, Mr. Lincoln and Mr. Trumbull, one an old-line Whig and the other an old-line Democrat, were hunting in partnership to elect a Legislature against the Democratic party. I canvassed the State that year from the time I returned home until the election came off, and spoke in every county that I could reach during that period. In the northern part of the State I found Lincoln's ally in the person of FRED DOUGLASS, THE NEGRO, preaching Abolition doctrines, while Lincoln was discussing the same principles down here, and Trumbull, a little farther down, was advocating the election of members to the Legislature who would act in concert with Lincoln's and Fred Douglass's friends. I witnessed an effort made at Chicago by Lincoln's then associates, and now supporters, to put Fred Douglass, the negro, on the stand, at a Democratic meeting, to reply to the illustrious General Cass when he was addressing the people there. They had the same negro hunting me down, and they now have a negro traversing the northern counties of the State and speaking in behalf of Lincoln. Lincoln knows that when we were at Freeport in joint discussion there was a distinguished colored friend of his there then who was on the stump for him, and who made a speech there the night before we spoke, and another the night after, a short distance from Freeport, in favor of Lincoln; and in order to show how much interest the colored brethren felt in the success of their brother Abe, I have with me here, and would read it if it would not occupy too much of my time, a speech made by Fred Douglass in Poughkeepsie, N. Y., a short time since, to a large convention in which he conjures all the friends of negro equality and negro citizenship to rally as one man around Abraham Lincoln, the perfect embodiment of their principles, and by all means to defeat Stephen A. Douglas. Thus you find that this Republican party in the northern part of the State had colored gentlemen for their advocates in 1854, in company with Lincoln and Trumbull, as they have now. When, in October, 1854, I went down to Springfield to attend the State Fair, I found the leaders of this party all assembled together under the title of an anti-Nebraska meeting. It was Black Republicans up north and anti-Nebraska at Springfield. I found Lovejoy, a high-priest of Abolitionism, and Lincoln, one of the leaders who was towing the old-line Whigs into the Abolition camp, and Trumbull, Sidney Breese, and Governor Reynolds, all making speeches against the Democratic party and myself, at the same place and in the same cause. The same men who are now fighting the

Democratic party and the regular Democratic nominees in this State were fighting us then. They
did not then acknowledge that they had become
Abolitionists, and many of them deny it now.
Breese, Dougherty, and Reynolds were then fighting
the Democracy under the title of anti-Nebraska men,
and now they are fighting the Democracy under the
pretence that they are *Simon pure* Democrats, saying
that they are authorized to have every office-holder
in Illinois beheaded who prefers the election of
Douglas to that of Lincoln or the success of the
Democratic ticket in preference to the Abolition
ticket for members of Congress, State officers, members of the Legislature, or any office in the State.
They canvassed the State against us in 1854, as they
are doing now, owning different names and different
principles in different localities, but having a common
object in view, viz.: the defeat of all men holding
national principles in opposition to this sectional
Abolition party. They carried the Legislature in
1854, and when it assembled in Springfield they proceeded to elect a United States Senator, all voting for
Lincoln, with one or two exceptions, which exceptions prevented them from quite electing him. And
why should they not elect him? Had not Trumbull
agreed that Lincoln should have Shields's place?
Had not the Abolitionists agreed to it? Was it not
the solemn compact, the condition on which Lincoln
agreed to Abolitionize the old Whigs, that he should
be Senator? Still, Trumbull, having control of a few
Abolitionized Democrats, would not allow them all
to vote for Lincoln on any one ballot, and thus kept

him for some time within one or two votes of an
election, until he worried out Lincoln's friends, and
compelled them to drop him and elect Trumbull, in
violation of the bargain. I desire to read you a
piece of testimony in confirmation of the notoriously
public facts which I have stated to you. Colonel
James H. Matheny, of Springfield, is, and for twenty
years has been, the confidential personal and political
friend and manager of Mr. Lincoln. Matheny is this
very day the candidate of the Republican or Abolition party for Congress against the gallant Major
Thos. L. Harris, in the Springfield District, and is
making speeches for Lincoln and against me. I will
read you the testimony of Matheny about this bargain between Lincoln and Trumbull when they
undertook to Abolitionize Whigs and Democrats
only four years ago. Matheny, being mad at Trumbull for having played a Yankee trick on Lincoln,
exposed the bargain in a public speech two years
ago, and I will read the published report of that
speech, the correctness of which Mr. Lincoln will
not deny:

"The Whigs, Abolitionists, Know-Nothings, and rene-
gade Democrats made a solemn compact for the purpose
of carrying this State against the Democracy, on this
plan: 1st, that they would all combine and elect Mr.
Trumbull to Congress, and thereby carry his district for
the Legislature, in order to throw all the strength that
could be obtained into that body against the Democrats;
2d, that when the Legislature should meet, the officers
of that body, such as Speaker, clerks, door-keepers, etc.
would be given to the Abolitionists; and, 3d, that the

Whigs were to have the United States Senator. That accordingly, in good faith, Trumbull was elected to Congress, and his district carried for the Legislature; and when it convened, the Abolitionists got all the officers of that body, and thus far the 'bond' was fairly executed. The Whigs, on their part, demanded the election of Abraham Lincoln to the United States Senate, that the bond might be fulfilled, the other parties to the contract having already secured to themselves all that was called for. But, in the most perfidious manner, they refused to elect Mr. Lincoln; and the mean, low-lived, sneaking Trumbull succeeded, by pleading all that was required by any party, in thrusting Lincoln aside, and foisting himself, an excrescence from the rotten bowels of the Democracy, into the United States Senate; and thus it has ever been, that an *honest* man makes a bad bargain when he conspires or contracts with rogues."

Lincoln's confidential friend Matheny thought that Lincoln made a bad bargain when he conspired with such rogues as Trumbull and the Abolitionists. I would like to know whether Lincoln had as high opinion of Trumbull's veracity when the latter agreed to support him for the Senate and then cheated him as he does now, when Trumbull comes forward and makes charges against me. You could not then prove Trumbull an honest man either by Lincoln, by Matheny, or by any of Lincoln's friends. They charged everywhere that Trumbull had cheated them out of the bargain, and Lincoln found sure enough that it was a *bad bargain* to contract and conspire with rogues.

And now I will explain to you what has been a mystery all over the State and Union—the reason

why Lincoln was nominated for the United States
Senate by the Black Republican Convention. You
know it has never been usual for any party or any
convention to nominate a candidate for United
States Senator. Probably this was the first time
that such a thing was ever done. The Black Republican Convention had not been called for that
purpose, but to nominate a State ticket, and every
man was surprised and many disgusted when Lincoln
was nominated. Archie Williams thought he was
entitled to it, Browning knew that he deserved it,
Wentworth was certain that he would get it, Peck
had hopes, Judd felt sure that he was the man, and
Palmer had claims and had made arrangements to
secure it; but to their utter amazement, Lincoln
was nominated by the Convention, and not only that,
but he received the nomination unanimously, by a
resolution declaring that Abraham Lincoln was "the
first, last, and only choice" of the Republican party.
How did this occur? Why, because they could not
get Lincoln's friends to make another bargain with
"rogues," unless the whole party would come up
as one man and pledge their honor that they would
stand by Lincoln first, last, and all the time, and
that he should not be cheated by Lovejoy this time,
as he was by Trumbull before. Thus, by passing this
resolution, the Abolitionists are all for him, Lovejoy
and Farnsworth are canvassing for him, Giddings is
ready to come here in his behalf, and the negro
speakers are already on the stump for him, and he is
sure not to be cheated this time. He would not go
into the arrangement until he got their bond for it,

and Trumbull is compelled now to take the stump,
get up false charges against me, and travel all over
the State to try and elect Lincoln, in order to keep
Lincoln's friends quiet about the bargain in which
Trumbull cheated them four years ago. You see,
now, why it is that Lincoln and Trumbull are so
mighty fond of each other. They have entered into
a conspiracy to break me down by these assaults upon
my public character, in order to draw my attention
from a fair exposure of the mode in which they
attempted to Abolitionize the old Whig and the old
Democratic parties and lead them captive into the
Abolition camp. Do you not all remember that
Lincoln went around here four years ago making
speeches to you, and telling that you should all go
for the Abolition ticket, and swearing that he was as
good a Whig as he ever was? and that Trumbull
went all over the State making pledges to the old
Democrats, and trying to coax them into the Abolition camp, swearing by his Maker, with the uplifted
hand, that he was still a Democrat, always intended
to be, and that never would he desert the Democratic party? He got your votes to elect an Abolition Legislature, which passed Abolition resolutions,
attempted to pass Abolition laws, and sustained
Abolitionists for office, State and National. Now
the same game is attempted to be played over again.
Then Lincoln and Trumbull made captives of the old
Whigs and old Democrats and carried them into the
Abolition camp, where Father Giddings, the high-
priest of Abolitionism, received and christened them
in the dark cause just as fast as they were brought in.

Giddings found the converts so numerous that he had to have assistance, and he sent for John P. Hale, N. P. Banks, Chase, and other Abolitionists, and they came on, and with Lovejoy and Fred Douglass, the negro, helped to baptize these new converts as Lincoln, Trumbull, Breese, Reynolds, and Dougherty could capture them and bring them within the Abolition clutch. Gentlemen, they are now around, making the same kind of speeches. Trumbull was down in Monroe County the other day, assailing me, and making a speech in favor of Lincoln; and I will show you under what notice his meeting was called. You see these people are Black Republicans or Abolitionists up north, while at Springfield to-day they dare not call their Convention "Republican," but are obliged to say "a Convention of all men opposed to the Democratic party"; and in Monroe County and lower Egypt Trumbull advertises their meetings as follows:

"A meeting of the Free Democracy will take place at Waterloo on Monday, September 21st inst., whereat Hon. Lyman Trumbull, Hon. John Baker, and others will address the people upon the different political topics of the day. Members of all parties are cordially invited to be present, and hear and determine for themselves.
                              "THE FREE DEMOCRACY.
"September 9, 1858."

Did you ever before hear of this new party, called the "Free Democracy"?

What object have these Black Republicans in changing their name in every county? They have

one name in the north, another in the centre, and
another in the south.   When I used to practise law
before my distinguished judicial friend whom I
recognize in the crowd before me, if a man was
charged with horse-stealing, and the proof showed
that he went by one name in Stephenson County,
another in Sangamon, a third in Monroe, and a fourth
in Randolph, we thought that the fact of his changing his name so often to avoid detection was pretty
strong evidence of his guilt.   I would like to know
why it is that this great Free-soil Abolition party is
not willing to avow the same name in all parts of the
State?   If this party believes that its course is just,
why does it not avow the same principles in the
North and in the South, in the East and in the West,
wherever the American flag waves over American
soil?

A voice: The party does not call itself Black Republican in the North.

Mr. DOUGLAS: Sir, if you will get a copy of the
paper published at Waukegan, fifty miles from
Chicago, which advocates the election of Mr. Lincoln,
and has his name flying at its mast-head, you will
find that it declares that "this paper is devoted to
the cause" of *Black Republicanism.*   I had a copy
of it, and intended to bring it down here into Egypt
to let you see what name the party rallied under up
in the northern part of the State, and to convince you
that their principles are as different in the two sec-
tions of the State as is their name.   I am sorry that
I have mislaid it and have not got it here.   Their
principles in the north are jet-black, in the centre

they are in color a decent mulatto, and in lower Egypt they are almost white. Why, I admired many of the white sentiments contained in Lincoln's speech at Jonesboro, and could not help but contrast them with the speeches of the same distinguished orator made in the northern part of the State. Down here he denies that the Black Republican party is opposed to the admission of any more slave States, under any circumstances, and says that they are willing to allow the people of each State, when it wants to come into the Union, to do just as it pleases on the question of slavery. In the north, you find Lovejoy, their candidate for Congress in the Bloomington District, Farnsworth, their candidate in the Chicago District, and Washburne, their candidate in the Galena District, all declaring that never will they consent, under any circumstances, to admit another slave State, even if the people want it. Thus, while they avow one set of principles up there, they avow another and entirely different set down here. And here let me recall to Mr. Lincoln the Scriptural quotation which he has applied to the Federal Government, that a house divided against itself cannot stand, and ask him how does he expect this Abolition party to stand when in one half of the State it advocates a set of principles which it has repudiated in the other half.

I am told that I have but eight minutes more. I would like to talk to you an hour and a half longer, but I will make the best use I can of the remaining eight minutes. Mr. Lincoln said in his first remarks that he was not in favor of the social and political equality of the negro with the white man.

Everywhere up north he has declared that he was not in favor of the social and political equality of the negro, but he would not say whether or not he was opposed to negroes voting and negro citizenship. I want to know whether he is for or against negro citizenship. He declared his utter opposition to the Dred Scott decision, and advanced as a reason that the court had decided that it was not possible for a negro to be a citizen under the Constitution of the United States. If he is opposed to the Dred Scott decision for that reason, he must be in favor of conferring the right and privilege of citizenship upon the negro. I have been trying to get an answer from him on that point, but have never yet obtained one, and I will show you why. In every speech he made in the north he quoted the Declaration of Independence to prove that all men were created equal, and insisted that the phrase "all men" included the negro as well as the white man, and that the equality rested upon divine law. Here is what he said on that point:

"I should like to know if, taking this old Declaration of Independence, which declares that all men are equal upon principle, and making exceptions to it, where will it stop? If one man says it does not mean a negro, why may not another say it does not mean some other man? If that Declaration is not the truth, let us get the statute book in which we find it and tear it out."

Lincoln maintains there that the Declaration of Independence asserts that the negro is equal to the white man, and that under divine law; and if he believes so it was rational for him to advocate negro citizenship, which when allowed puts the negro on an equality under the law. I say to you in all frankness, gentlemen, that in my opinion a negro is not a citizen, cannot be, and ought not to be under the Constitution of the United States. I will not even qualify my opinion to meet the declaration of one of the judges of the Supreme Court in the Dred Scott case, that "a negro descended from African parents, who was imported into this country as a slave, is not a citizen, and cannot be." I say that this government was established on the white basis. It was made by white men for the benefit of white men and their posterity forever, and never should be administered by any except white men. I declare that a negro ought not to be a citizen, whether his parents were imported into this country as slaves or not, or whether or not he was born here. It does not depend upon the place a negro's parents were born, or whether they were slaves or not, but upon the fact that he is a negro, belonging to a race incapable of self-government, and for that reason ought not to be on an equality with white men.

My friends, I am sorry that I have not time to pursue this argument further, as I might have done but for the fact that Mr. Lincoln compelled me to occupy a portion of my time in repelling those gross slanders and falsehoods that Trumbull has invented against me and put in circulation. In conclusion, let me ask you why should this government be divided by a geographical line—arraying all men North in one great hostile party against all men South? Mr.

Lincoln tells you in his speech at Springfield that a house divided against itself cannot stand; that this government divided into free and slave States cannot endure permanently; that they must either be all free or all slave; all one thing or all the other. Why cannot this government endure divided into free and slave States, as our fathers made it? When this government was established by Washington, Jefferson, Madison, Jay, Hamilton, Franklin, and the other sages and patriots of that day, it was composed of free States and slave States, bound together by one common Constitution. We have existed and prospered from that day to this thus divided, and have increased with a rapidity never before equalled, in wealth, the extension of territory, and all the elements of power and greatness, until we have become the first nation on the face of the globe. Why can we not thus continue to prosper? We can if we will live up to and execute the government upon those principles upon which our fathers established it. During the whole period of our existence Divine Providence has smiled upon us, and showered upon our nation richer and more abundant blessings than have ever been conferred upon any other.

MR. LINCOLN'S REJOINDER.

FELLOW-CITIZENS: It follows as a matter of course that a half-hour answer to a speech of an hour and a half can be but a very hurried one. I shall only be

able to touch upon a few of the points suggested by
Judge Douglas, and give them a brief attention,
while I shall have to totally omit others for the want
of time.

Judge Douglas has said to you that he has not
been able to get from me an answer to the question
whether I am in favor of negro citizenship. So far
as I know the Judge never asked me the question
before. He shall have no occasion to ever ask it
again, for I tell him very frankly that I am not in
favor of negro citizenship. This furnishes me an
occasion for saying a few words upon the subject.
I mentioned in a certain speech of mine, which has
been printed, that the Supreme Court had decided
that a negro could not possibly be made a citizen;
and without saying what was my ground of complaint in regard to that, or whether I had any ground
of complaint, Judge Douglas has from that thing
manufactured nearly everything that he ever says
about my disposition to produce an equality between
the negroes and the white people. If any one will
read my speech, he will find I mentioned that as one of
the points decided in the course of the Supreme Court
opinions, but I did not state what objection I had to it.
But Judge Douglas tells the people what my objection
was when I did not tell them myself. Now, my opinion is that the different States have the power to
make a negro a citizen under the Constitution of the
United States if they choose. The Dred Scott decision decides that they have not that power. If the
State of Illinois had that power, I should be opposed to
the exercise of it. That is all I have to say about it.

Judge Douglas has told me that he heard my speeches north and my speeches south; that he had heard me at Ottawa and at Freeport in the north and recently at Jonesboro in the south, and there was a very different cast of sentiment in the speeches made at the different points. I will not charge upon Judge Douglas that he wilfully misrepresents me, but I call upon every fair-minded man to take these speeches and read them, *and I dare him to point out any difference between my speeches north and south.* While I am here perhaps I ought to say a word, if I have the time, in regard to the latter portion of the Judge's speech, which was a sort of declamation in reference to my having said I entertained the belief that this government would not endure half slave and half free. I have said so, and I did not say it without what seemed to me to be good reasons. It perhaps would require more time than I have now to set forth these reasons in detail; but let me ask you a few questions. Have we ever had any peace on this slavery question? When are we to have peace upon it, if it is kept in the position it now occupies? How are we ever to have peace upon it? That is an important question. To be sure, if we will all stop, and allow Judge Douglas and his friends to march on in their present career until they plant the institution all over the nation, here and wherever else our flag waves, and we acquiesce in it, there will be peace. But let me ask Judge Douglas how he is going to get the people to do that? They have been wrangling over this question for at least forty years. This was the cause of the agitation resulting in the Missouri

Compromise; this produced the troubles at the
annexation of Texas, in the acquisition of the territory acquired in the Mexican War. Again, this was
the trouble which was quieted by the Compromise of
1850, when it was settled "*forever* " as both the great
political parties declared in their National Conventions. That "forever" turned out to be just four
years, *when Judge Douglas himself reopened it.*
When is it likely to come to an end? He introduced
the Nebraska Bill in 1854 to put *another end* to the
slavery agitation. He promised that it would fin-
ish it all up immediately, and he has never made a
speech since, until he got into a quarrel with the
President about the Lecompton Constitution, in
which he has not declared that we are *just at the end*
of the slavery agitation. But in one speech, I think
last winter, he did say that he did n't quite see when
the end of the slavery agitation would come. Now
he tells us again that it is all over and the people of
Kansas have voted down the Lecompton Constitution. How is it over? That was only one of the
attempts at putting an end to the slavery agitation
—one of these "final settlements." Is Kansas in the
Union? Has she formed a constitution that she is
likely to come in under? Is not the slavery agitation
still an open question in that Territory? Has the
voting down of that constitution put an end to all the
trouble? Is that more likely to settle it than every
one of these previous attempts to settle the slavery
agitation? Now, at this day in the history of the
world we can no more foretell where the end of this
slavery agitation will be than we can see the end of

the world itself. The Nebraska-Kansas Bill was introduced four years and a half ago, and if the agitation is ever to come to an end we may say we are four years and a half nearer the end. So, too, we can say we are four years and a half nearer the end of the world, and we can just as clearly see the end of the world as we can see the end of this agitation. The Kansas settlement did not conclude it. If Kansas should sink to-day, and leave a great vacant space in the earth's surface, this vexed question would still be among us. I say, then, there is no way of putting an end to the slavery agitation amongst us but to put it back upon the basis where our fathers placed it; no way but to keep it out of our new Territories,—to restrict it forever to the old States where it now exists. Then the public mind *will* rest in the belief that it is in the course of ultimate extinction. That is one way of putting an end to the slavery agitation.

The other way is for us to surrender and let Judge Douglas and his friends have their way and plant slavery over all the States; cease speaking of it as in any way a wrong; regard slavery as one of the common matters of property, and speak of negroes as we do of our horses and cattle. But while it drives on in its state of progress as it is now driving, and as it has driven for the last five years, I have ventured the opinion, and I say to-day, that we will have no end to the slavery agitation until it takes one turn or the other. I do not mean that when it takes a turn toward ultimate extinction it will be in a day, nor in a year, nor in two years. I do not suppose that in the most peaceful way ultimate extinction would occur in less than a hundred years at least; but that it will occur in the best way for both races, in God's own good time, I have no doubt. But, my friends, I have used up more of my time than I intended on this point.

Now, in regard to this matter about Trumbull and myself having made a bargain to sell out the entire Whig and Democratic parties in 1854: Judge Douglas brings forward no evidence to sustain his charge, except the speech Matheny is said to have made in 1856, in which he told a cock-and-bull story of that sort, upon the same moral principles that Judge Douglas tells it here to-day. This is the simple truth. I do not care greatly for the story, but this is the truth of it: and I have twice told Judge Douglas to his face that from beginning to end there is not one word of truth in it. I have called upon him for the proof, and he does not at all meet me as Trumbull met him upon that of which we were just talking, by producing the record. He did n't bring the record because there was no record for him to bring. When he asks if I am ready to indorse Trumbull's veracity after he has broken a bargain with me, I reply that if Trumbull *had* broken a bargain with me I would not be likely to indorse his veracity; but I am ready to indorse his veracity because *neither in that thing, nor in any other, in all the years that I have known Lyman Trumbull, have I known him to fail of his word or tell a falsehood large or small.* It is for that reason that I indorse Lyman Trumbull.

Mr. JAMES BROWN (*Douglas postmaster*): What does Ford's History say about him?

Mr. LINCOLN: Some gentleman asks me what Ford's History says about him. My own recollection is that Ford speaks of Trumbull in very disrespectful terms in several portions of his book, *and that he talks a great deal worse of Judge Douglas.* I refer you, sir, to the History for examination.

Judge Douglas complains at considerable length about a disposition on the part of Trumbull and myself to attack him personally. I want to attend to that suggestion a moment. I don't want to be unjustly accused of dealing illiberally or unfairly with an adversary, either in court or in a political canvass or anywhere else. I would despise myself if I supposed myself ready to deal less liberally with an adversary than I was willing to be treated myself. Judge Douglas in a general way, without putting it in a direct shape, revives the old charge against me in reference to the Mexican War. He does not take the responsibility of putting it in a very definite form, but makes a general reference to it. That charge is more than ten years old. He complains of Trumbull and myself because he says we bring charges against him one or two years old. He knows, too, that in regard to the Mexican War story the more respectable papers of his own party throughout the State have been compelled to take it back and acknowledge that it was a lie.

[Here Mr. LINCOLN turned to the crowd on the platform, and, selecting Hon. ORLANDO B. FICKLIN, led him forward and said:]

I do not mean to do anything with Mr. Ficklin except to present his face and tell you that *he*

personally knows it to be a lie! He was a member of
Congress at the only time I was in Congress, and
[Ficklin] knows that whenever there was an attempt
to procure a vote of mine which would indorse the
origin and justice of the war, I refused to give such
indorsement and voted against it; but I never
voted against the supplies for the army, and he
knows, as well as Judge Douglas, that whenever
a dollar was asked by way of compensation or otherwise for the benefit of the soldiers *I gave all the votes
that Ficklin or Douglas did, and perhaps more.*

Mr. FICKLIN: My friends, I wish to say this in
reference to the matter: Mr. Lincoln and myself
are just as good personal friends as Judge Douglas
and myself. In reference to this Mexican War, my recollection is that when Ashmun's resolution [amend-
ment] was offered by Mr. Ashmun of Massachusetts,
in which he declared that the Mexican War was
unnecessary and unconstitutionally commenced by
the President —my recollection is that Mr. Lincoln
voted for that resolution.

Mr. LINCOLN: That is the truth. Now, you all
remember that was a resolution censuring the President for the manner in which the war was *begun.*
You know they have charged that I voted against
the supplies, by which I starved the soldiers who
were out fighting the battles of their country. I say
that Ficklin knows it is false. When that charge
was brought forward by the Chicago *Times*, the
Springfield *Register* [Douglas's organ] reminded the
Times that the charge really applied to John Henry;
and I do know that John Henry *is now making*

speeches and fiercely battling for Judge Douglas. If the Judge now says that he offers this as a sort of set-off to what I said to-day in reference to Trumbull's charge, then I remind him that he made this charge before I said a word about Trumbull's. He brought this forward at Ottawa, the first time we met face to face; and in the opening speech that Judge Douglas made he attacked me in regard to a matter ten years old. Is n't he a pretty man to be whining about people making charges against him only *two* years old!

The Judge thinks it is altogether wrong that I should have dwelt upon this charge of Trumbull's at all. I gave the apology for doing so in my opening speech. Perhaps it did n't fix your attention. I said that when Judge Douglas was speaking at places where I spoke on the succeeding day he used very harsh language about this charge. Two or three times afterward I said I had confidence in Judge Trumbull's veracity and intelligence; and my own opinion was, from what I knew of the character of Judge Trumbull, that he would vindicate his position and prove whatever he had stated to be true. This I repeated two or three times; and then I dropped it, without saying anything more on the subject for weeks —perhaps a month. I passed it by without noticing it at all till I found, at Jacksonville, Judge Douglas in the plenitude of his power is not willing to answer Trumbull and let me alone, but he comes out there and uses this language: "He should not hereafter occupy his time in refuting such charges made by Trumbull but that, Lincoln having indorsed the character of Trumbull for veracity, he should hold him [Lincoln] responsible for the slanders." What was Lincoln to do? Did he not do right, when he had the fit opportunity of meeting Judge Douglas here, to tell him he was ready for the responsibility? I ask a candid audience whether in doing thus Judge Douglas was not the assailant rather than I? Here I meet him face to face, and say I am ready to take the responsibility, so far as it rests on me.

Having done so I ask the attention of this audience to the question whether I have succeeded in sustaining the charge, and whether Judge Douglas has at all succeeded in rebutting it? You all heard me call upon him to say *which of these pieces of evidence was a forgery.* Does he say that what I present here as a copy of the original Toombs bill is a forgery? Does he say that what I present as a copy of the bill reported by himself is a forgery, or what is presented as a transcript from the *Globe* of the quotations from Bigler's speech is a forgery? Does he say the quotations from his own speech are forgeries? Does he say this transcript from Trumbull's speech is a forgery? ["He did n't deny one of them."] *I would then like to know how it comes about that when each piece of a story is true the whole story turns out false.* I take it these people have some sense; they see plainly that Judge Douglas is playing cuttle-fish, —a small species of fish that has no mode of defending itself when pursued except by throwing out a black fluid, which makes the water so dark the enemy cannot see it, and thus it escapes. Ain't the Judge playing the cuttle-fish?

Now, I would ask very special attention to the consideration of Judge Douglas's speech at Jacksonville; and when you shall read his speech of to-day, I ask you to watch closely and see which of these pieces of testimony, every one of which he says is a forgery, he has shown to be such. *Not one of them has he shown to be a forgery.* Then I ask the original question, if each of the pieces of testimony is true, *how is it possible that the whole is a falsehood?*

In regard to Trumbull's charge that he [Douglas] inserted a provision into the bill to prevent the constitution being submitted to the people, what was his answer? He comes here and reads from the *Congressional Globe* to show that on his motion that provision was struck out of the bill. Why, Trumbull has not said it was not stricken out, but Trumbull says he [Douglas] put it in; and it is no answer to the charge to say he afterwards took it out. Both are perhaps true. It was in regard to that thing precisely that I told him he had dropped the cub. Trumbull shows you that by his introducing the bill it was his cub. It is no answer to that assertion to call Trumbull a liar merely because he did not specially say that Douglas struck it out. Suppose that were the case, does it answer Trumbull? I assert that you [pointing to an individual] are here to-day, and you undertake to prove me a liar by showing that you were in Mattoon yesterday. I say that you took your hat off your head, and you prove me a liar by putting it on your head. That is the whole force of Douglas's argument.

Now, I want to come back to my original question.

Trumbull says that Judge Douglas had a bill with a provision in it for submitting a constitution to be made to a vote of the people of Kansas. Does Judge Douglas deny that fact? Does he deny that the provision which Trumbull reads was put in that bill? Then Trumbull says he struck it out. Does he dare to deny that? He does not, and I have the right to repeat the question,—*Why Judge Douglas took it out?* Bigler has said there was a combination of certain senators, among whom he did not include Judge Douglas, by which it was agreed that the Kansas Bill should have a clause in it not to have the constitution formed under it submitted to a vote of the people. He did not say that Douglas was among them, but we prove by another source that about the same time Douglas comes into the Senate *with that provision stricken out of the bill.* Although Bigler cannot say they were all working in concert, yet it looks very much as if the thing was agreed upon and done with a mutual understanding after the conference; and while we do not know that it was absolutely so, yet it looks so probable that we have a right to call upon the man who knows the true reason why it was done *to tell what the true reason was.* When he will not tell what the true reason was, he stands in the attitude of an accused thief who has stolen goods in his possession, and when called to account refuses to tell where he got them. Not only is this the evidence, but when he comes in with the bill having the provision stricken out, he tells us in a speech, not then but since, that these alterations and modifications in the bill *had been made by* HIM, *in consultation with*

Toombs, the originator of the bill. He tells us the same to-day. He says there were certain modifications made in the bill in committee that he did not vote for. I ask you to remember, while certain amendments were made which he disapproved of, but which a majority of the committee voted in, he has himself told us that in this particular *the alterations and modifications were made by him, upon consultation with Toombs.* We have his own word that these alterations were made *by him,* and not by the committee. Now, I ask, what is the reason Judge Douglas is so chary about coming to the exact question? What is the reason he will not tell you anything about HOW it was made, BY WHOM it was made, or that he remembers it being made at all? Why does he stand playing upon the meaning of words and quibbling around the edges of the evidence? If he can explain all this, but leaves it unexplained, I have the right to infer that Judge Douglas understood it was the purpose of his party, in engineering that bill through, to make a constitution, and have Kansas come into the Union with that constitution, *without its being submitted to a vote of the poeple.* If he will explain his action on this question, by giving a *better reason* for the facts that happened than he has done, it will be satisfactory. But until he does that—until he gives a better or more plausible reason than he has offered against the evidence in the case —*I suggest to him it will not avail him at all that he swells himself up, takes on dignity, and calls people liars.* Why, sir, there is not a word in Trumbull's speech that depends on Trumbull's veracity at all.

He has only arrayed the evidence and told you what follows as a matter of reasoning. There is not a statement in the whole speech that depends on Trumbull's word. If you have ever studied geometry, you remember that by a course of reasoning Euclid proves that all the angles in a triangle are equal to two right angles. Euclid has shown you how to work it out. Now, if you undertake to disprove that proposition, and to show that it is erroneous, would you prove it to be false by calling Euclid a liar? They tell me that my time is out, and therefore I close.

EXTRACT FROM MR. TRUMBULL'S SPEECH MADE AT ALTON,
REFERRED TO BY MR. LINCOLN IN HIS
OPENING AT CHARLESTON.

I come now to another extract from a speech of Mr. Douglas, made at Beardstown, and reported in the *Missouri Republican*. This extract has reference to a statement made by me at Chicago, wherein I charged that an agreement had been entered into by the very persons now claiming credit for opposing a constitution not submitted to the people, to have a constitution formed and put in force without giving the people of Kansas an opportunity to pass upon it. Without meeting this charge, which I substantiated by a reference to the record, my colleague is reported to have said:

"For when this charge was made once in a much milder form, in the Senate of the United States, I did brand it as a lie in the presence of Mr. Trumbull, and Mr. Trumbull sat and heard it thus branded, without daring to say it was true. I tell you he knew it to be false when he uttered it at Chicago; and yet he says he is going to cram the lie down his throat until he should cry Enough. The miserable, craven-hearted wretch! He would rather have both ears cut off than to use that language in my presence, where I could call him to account. I see the object is to draw me into a personal controversy, with the hope thereby of concealing from the public the enormity of the principles to which they are committed. I shall not allow much of my time in this canvass to be occupied by these personal assaults: I have none to make on Mr. Lincoln; I have none to make on Mr. Trumbull; I have none to make on any other political opponent. If I cannot stand on my own public record, on my own private and public character as history will record it, I will not attempt to rise by traducing the character of other men. I will not make a blackguard of myself by imitating the course they have pursued against me. I have no charges to make against them."

This is a singular statement, taken altogether. After indulging in language which would disgrace a loafer in the filthiest purlieus of a fish market, he winds up by saying that he will not make a blackguard of himself, that he has no charges to make against me. So I suppose he considers that to say of another that he knew a thing to be false when he uttered it, that he was a "miserable, craven-hearted wretch," does not amount to a personal assault, and does not make a man a blackguard. A discriminating public will judge of that for themselves; but as he says he has "no charges to make on Mr. Trumbull," I suppose politeness requires I should believe him. At the risk of again offending this mighty man of war, and losing something more than my ears, I shall have the audacity to again read the record upon him, and prove and pin upon him, so that he cannot escape it, the truth

of every word I uttered at Chicago. You, fellow-citizens, are the judges to determine whether I do this. My colleague says he is willing to stand on his public record. By that shall he be tried; and if he had been able to discriminate between the exposure of a public act by the record, and a personal attack upon the individual, he would have discovered that there was nothing personal in my Chicago remarks, unless the condemnation of himself by his own public record is personal; and then you must judge who is most to blame for the torture his public record inflicts upon him—he for making, or I for reading it after it was made. As an individual, I care very little about Judge Douglas one way or the other. It is his public acts with which I have to do, and if they condemn, disgrace, and consign him to oblivion, he has only himself, not me, to blame.

Now, the charge is that there was a plot entered into to have a constitution formed for Kansas, and put in force, without giving the people an opportunity to pass upon it, and that Mr. Douglas was in the plot. That is as susceptible of proof by the record as is the fact that the State of Minnesota was admitted into the Union at the last session of Congress.

On the 25th of June, 1856, a bill was pending in the United States Senate to authorize the people of Kansas to form a constitution and come into the Union. On that day Mr. Toombs offered an amendment which he intended to propose to the bill, which was ordered to be printed, and, with the original bill and other amendments, recommended to the Committee on Territories, of which Mr. Douglas was chairman. This amendment of Mr. Toombs, printed by order of the Senate, and a copy of which I have here present, provided for the appointment of commissioners who were to take a census of Kansas,

divide the Territory into election districts, and super-
intend the election of delegates to form a constitution,
and contains a clause in the 18th section which I will
read to you, requiring the constitution which should be
formed to be submitted to the people for adoption. It
reads as follows:

"That the following propositions be and the same are
hereby offered to the said Convention of the people of
Kansas, when formed, for their free acceptance or rejection, which, if accepted by the Convention, and
ratified by the people at the election for the adoption of
the constitution, shall be obligatory on the United States,
and upon the said State of Kansas," etc.

It has been contended by some of the newspaper press
that this section did not require the constitution which
should be formed to be submitted to the people for approval, and that it was only the land propositions which
were to be submitted. You will observe the language
is that the propositions are to be "ratified by the people
at the election for the adoption of the constitution."
Would it have been possible to ratify the land propositions "at the election for the adoption of the constitution," unless such an election was to be held?

When one thing is required by a contract or law to be
done, the doing of which is made dependent upon and
cannot be performed without the doing of some other
thing, is not that other thing just as much required by
the contract or law as the first? It matters not in what
part of the act, nor in what phraseology, the intention of
the Legislature is expressed, so you can clearly ascertain
what it is; and whenever that intention is ascertained
from an examination of the language used, such intention
is part of and a requirement of the law. Can any candid,
fair-minded man read the section I have quoted, and say

that the intention to have the constitution which should be formed submitted to the people for their adoption, is not clearly expressed? In my judgment, there can be no controversy among honest men upon a proposition so plain as this. Mr. Douglas has never pretended to deny, so far as I am aware, that the Toombs amendment, as originally introduced, did require a submission of the constitution to the people. This amendment of Mr. Toombs's was referred to the committee of which Mr. Douglas was chairman, and reported back by him on the 30th of June, with the words "and ratified by the people at the election for the adoption of the constitution " stricken out. I have here a copy of the bill as reported back by Mr. Douglas, to substantiate the statement I make. Various other alterations were also made in the bill, to which I shall presently have occasion to call attention. There was no other clause in the original Toombs bill requiring a submission of the constitution to the people than the one I have read, and there was no clause whatever, after that was struck out, in the bill, as reported back by Judge Douglas, requiring a submission. I will now introduce a witness whose testimony cannot be impeached, he acknowledging himself to have been one of the conspirators and privy to the fact about which he testifies.

Senator Bigler, alluding to the Toombs bill, as it was called, and which, after sundry amendments, passed the Senate, and to the propriety of submitting the constitution which should be formed to a vote of the people, made the following statement in his place in the Senate, December 9th, 1857. I read from part 1, *Congressional Globe* of last session, paragraph 21:

"I was present when that subject was discussed by senators, before the bill was introduced, and the question was raised and discussed whether the constitution, when formed, should be submitted to a vote of the people. It was held by the most intelligent on the subject that in view of all the difficulties surrounding that Territory, the danger of any experiment at that time of a popular vote, it would be better that there should be no such provision in the Toombs bill; and it was my understanding, in all the intercourse I had, that that convention would make a constitution and send it here, without submitting it to the popular vote."

In speaking of this meeting again on the 21st December, 1857 (*Congressional Globe*, same volume, page 113), Senator Bigler said:

"Nothing was farther from my mind than to allude to any social or confidential interview. The meeting was not of that character. Indeed, it was semi-official, and called to promote the public good. My recollection was clear that I left the conference under the impression that it had been deemed best to adopt measures to admit Kansas as a State through the agency of one popular election, and that for delegates to the Convention. This impression was the stronger, because I thought the spirit of the bill infringed upon the doctrine of non-intervention, to which I had great aversion; but with the hope of accomplishing great good, and as no movement had been made in that direction in the Territory, I waived this objection, and concluded to support the measure. I have a few items of testimony, as to the correctness of these impressions, and with their submission I shall be content. I have before me the bill reported by the Senator from Illinois, on the 7th of March, 1856, providing for the admission of Kansas as a State, the third section of which reads as follows:

"'That the following propositions be, and the same

are hereby offered to the said Convention of the people of Kansas, when formed, for their free acceptance or rejection; which, if accepted by the Convention and ratified by the people at the election for the adoption of the constitution, shall be obligatory upon the United States and upon the said State of Kansas.'

"The bill read in place by the Senator from Georgia, on the 25th of June, and referred to the Committee on Territories, contained the same section, word for word. Both these bills were under consideration at the conference referred to; but, sir, when the Senator from Illinois reported the Toombs bill to the Senate, with amendments, the next morning, it did not contain that portion of the third section which indicated to the Convention that the constitution should be approved by the people. The words 'and ratified by the people at the election for the adoption of the constitution' had been stricken out."

I am not now seeking to prove that Douglas was in the plot to force a constitution upon Kansas without allowing the people to vote directly upon it. I shall attend to that branch of the subject by and by. My object now is to prove the existence of the plot, what the design was, and I ask if I have not already done so. Here are the facts:

The introduction of a bill on the 7th of March, 1856, providing for the calling of a convention in Kansas to form a State constitution, and providing that the constitution should be submitted to the people for adoption; an amendment to this bill, proposed by Mr. Toombs, containing the same requirement; a reference of these various bills to the Committee on Territories; a consultation of senators to determine whether it was advisable to have the constitution submitted for ratification; the determination that it was not advisable; and a

report of the bill back to the Senate next morning, with
the clause providing for the submission stricken out.
Could evidence be more complete to establish the first
part of the charge I have made of a plot having been
entered into by somebody, to have a constitution adopted
without submitting it to the people?

Now for the other part of the charge, that Judge
Douglas was in this plot, whether knowingly or igno-
rantly is not material to my purpose.   The charge is that
he was an instrument co-operating in the project to have
a constitution formed and put into operation, without
affording the people an opportunity to pass upon it.
The first evidence to sustain the charge is the fact that
he reported back the Toombs amendment with the
clause providing for the submission stricken out,—this
in connection with his speech in the Senate on the 9th
of December, 1857 (*Congressional Globe*, part 1, page
14), wherein he stated:

"That during the last Congress I [Mr. Douglas] reported a bill from the Committee on Territories, to
authorize the people of Kansas to assemble and form a
constitution for themselves. Subsequently the Senator
from Georgia (Mr. Toombs) brought forward a substitute for my bill, which, after having been modified by
him and myself in consultation, was passed by the
Senate."

This of itself ought to be sufficient to show that my
colleague was an instrument in the plot to have a constitution put in force without submitting it to the people,
and to forever close his mouth from attempting to deny.
No man can reconcile his acts and former declarations
with his present denial, and the only charitable conclusion would be that he was being used by others without
knowing it. Whether he is entitled to the benefit of

even this excuse, you must judge on a candid hearing of
the facts I shall present. When the charge was first
made in the United States Senate, by Mr. Bigler, that
my colleague had voted for an Enabling Act which
put a government in operation without submitting the
constitution to the people, my colleague (*Congressional
Globe*, last session, part 1, page 24) stated:

"I will ask the Senator to show me an intimation from
any one member of the Senate, in the whole debate on the
Toombs bill, and in the Union from any quarter, that
the constitution was not be to submitted to the people.
I will venture to say that on all sides of the chamber it
was so understood at the time. If the opponents of the
bill had understood it was not, they would have made
the point on it; and if they had made it, we should certainly have yielded to it, and put in the clause. That
is a discovery made since the President found out that it
was not safe to take it for granted that that would be
done which ought in fairness to have been done."

I knew at the time this statement was made that I had
urged the very objection to the Toombs bill two years
before, that it did not provide for the submission of the
constitution. You will find my remarks, made on the
2nd of July, 1856, in the appendix to the *Congressional
Globe* of that year, page 179, urging this very objection.
Do you ask why I did not expose him at the time? I
will tell you: Mr. Douglas was then doing good service
against the Lecompton iniquity. The Republicans were
then engaged in a hand-to-hand fight with the National
Democracy to prevent the bringing of Kansas into the
Union as a slave State against the wishes of its inhabitants, and of course I was unwilling to turn our guns
from the common enemy to strike down an ally. Judge
Douglas, however, on the same day, and in the same

debate, probably recollecting, or being reminded of, the fact that I had objected to the Toombs bill when pending, that it did not provide for the submission of the constitution to the people, made another statement, which is to be found in the same volume of the *Congressional Globe*, page 22, in which he says:

"That the bill was silent on the subject is true, and my attention was called to that about the time it was passed; and I took the fair construction to be, that powers not delegated were reserved, and that of course the constitution would be submitted to the people."

Whether this statement is consistent with the statement just before made, that had the point been made it would have been yielded to, or that it was a new discovery, you will determine; for if the public records do not convict and condemn him, he may go uncondemned, so far as I am concerned. I make no use here of the testimony of Senator Bigler to show that Judge Douglas must have been privy to the consultation held at his house, when it was determined not to submit the constitution to the people, because Judge Douglas denies it, and I wish to use his own acts and declarations, which are abundantly sufficient for my purpose.

I come to a piece of testimony which disposes of all these various pretences which have been set up for striking out of the original Toombs proposition the clause requiring a submission of the constitution to the people, and shows that it was not done either by accident, by inadvertence, or because it was believed that, the bill being silent on the subject, the constitution would necessarily be submitted to the people for approval. What will you think, after listening to the facts already presented, to show that there was a design with those who concocted the Toombs bill, as amended, not to submit the constitu-

tion to the people, if I now bring before you the amended
bill as Judge Douglas reported it back, and show the
clause of the original bill requiring submission was not
only struck out, but that other clauses were inserted in
the bill, putting it absolutely out of the power of the
Convention to submit the constitution to the people for
approval, had they desired to do so? If I can produce such evidence as that, will you not all agree
that it clinches and establishes forever all I charged at
Chicago, and more too?

I propose now to furnish that evidence. It will be
remembered that Mr. Toombs's bill provided for holding
an election for delegates to form a constitution under
the supervision of commissioners to be appointed by the
President; and in the bill as reported back by Judge
Douglas, these words, *not to be found in the original bill*,
are inserted at the close of the 11th section, viz.:

"And until the complete execution of this Act, no
other election shall be held in said Territory."

This clause put it out of the power of the Convention
to refer to the people for adoption; it absolutely prohibited the holding of any other election than that for the
election of delegates, till that act was completely executed, which would not have been until Kansas was
admitted as a State, or at all events till her constitution
was fully prepared and ready for submission to Congress
for admission. Other amendments reported by Judge
Douglas to the original Toombs bill clearly show that the
intention was to enable Kansas to become a State without any further action than simply a resolution of admission. The amendment reported by Mr. Douglas, that
"until the next Congressional apportionment, the said
State shall have one representative," clearly shows this,
no such provision being contained in the original Toombs

bill. For what other earthly purpose could the clause
to prevent any other election in Kansas, except that of
delegates, till it was admitted as a State, have been inserted, except to prevent a submission of the constitution, when formed, to the people?

The Toombs bill did not pass in the exact shape in
which Judge Douglas reported it. Several amendments
were made to it in the Senate. I am now dealing with
the action of Judge Douglas as connected with that bill,
and speak of the bill as he recommended it. The facts I
have stated in regard to this matter appear upon the
records, which I have here present to show to any man
who wishes to look at them. They establish beyond the
power of controversy all the charges I have made, and
show that Judge Douglas was made use of as an instrument by others, or else knowingly was a party to the
scheme, to have a government put in force over the people
of Kansas without giving them an opportunity to pass
upon it. That others high in position in the so-called
Democratic party were parties to such a scheme is confessed by Governor Bigler; and the only reason why the
scheme was not carried, and Kansas long ago forced into
the Union as a slave State, is the fact, that the Republicans were sufficiently strong in the House of Representatives to defeat the measure.

———

EXTRACT FROM MR. DOUGLAS'S SPEECH MADE AT JACKSON-
VILLE, AND REFERRED TO BY MR. LINCOLN
IN HIS OPENING AT CHARLESTON.

I have been reminded by a friend behind me that there
is another topic upon which there has been a desire expressed that I should speak. I am told that Mr. Lyman
Trumbull, who has the good fortune to hold a seat in the

United States Senate, in violation of the bargain between him and Lincoln, was here the other day and occupied his time in making certain charges against me, involving, if they be true, moral turpitude. I am also informed that the charges he made here were substantially the same as those made by him in the city of Chicago, which were printed in the newspapers of that city. I now propose to answer those charges and to annihilate every pretext that an honest man has. ever had for repeating them.

In order that I may meet these charges fairly, I will read them, as made by Mr. Trumbull, in his Chicago speech, in his own language. He says:

"Now, fellow-citizens, I make the distinct charge that there was a preconcerted arrangement and plot entered into by the very men who now claim credit for opposing a constitution not submitted to the people, to have a constitution formed and put in force without giving the people an opportunity to pass upon it. This, my friends, is a serious charge, but I charge it to-night that the very men who traverse the country under banners proclaiming popular sovereignty, by design concocted a bill on purpose to force a constitution upon that people."

Again, speaking to some one in the crowd, he says:

"And you want to satisfy yourself that he was in the plot to force a constitution upon that people? I will satisfy you. I will cram the truth down any honest man's throat until he cannot deny it, and to the man who does deny it I will cram the lie down his throat till he shall cry, 'Enough!' It is preposterous; it is the most damnable effrontery that man ever put on to conceal a scheme to defraud and cheat the people out of their rights, and then claim credit for it."

That is polite and decent language for a Senator of the

6

United States. Remember that that language was used without any provocation whatever from me. I had not alluded to him in any manner in any speech that I had made, hence without provocation. As soon as he sets his foot within the State, he makes the direct charge that I was a party to a plot to force a constitution upon the people of Kansas against their will, and, knowing that it would be denied, he talks about cramming the lie down the throat of any man who shall deny it, until he cries, "Enough!"

Why did he take it for granted that it would be denied, unless he knew it to be false? Why did he deem it necessary to make a threat in advance that he would "cram the lie" down the throat of any man that should deny it? I have no doubt that the entire Abolition party consider it very polite for Mr. Trumbull to go round uttering calumnies of that kind, bullying, and talking of cramming lies down men's throats; but if I deny any of his lies by calling him a liar, they are shocked at the indecency of the language; hence, to-day, instead of calling him a liar, I intend to prove that he is one.

I wish, in the first place, to refer to the evidence adduced by Trumbull, at Chicago, to sustain his charge. He there declared that Mr. Toombs, of Georgia, introduced a bill into Congress authorizing the people of Kansas to form a constitution and come into the Union, that when introduced it contained a clause requiring the constitution to be submitted to the people, and that I struck out the words of that clause.

Suppose it were true that there was such a clause in the bill, and that I struck it out, is that proof of a plot to force a constitution upon a people against their will? Bear in mind that from the days of George Washington to the Administration of Franklin Pierce, there had never been passed by Congress a bill requiring the submission of a constitution to the people. If Trumbull's charge, that I struck out that clause, were true, it would only prove that I had reported the bill in the exact shape of every bill of like character that passed under Washington, Jefferson, Madison, Monroe, Jackson, or any other President, to the time of the then present Administration. I ask you, would that be evidence of a design to force a constitution on a people against their will? If it were so, it would be evidence against Washington, Jefferson, Madison, Jackson, Van Buren, and every other President.

But, upon examination, it turns out that the Toombs bill never did contain a clause requiring the constitution to be submitted. Hence no such clause was ever stricken out, by me or anybody else. It is true, however, that the Toombs bill and its authors all took it for granted that the constitution would be submitted. There had never been, in the history of this government, any attempt made to force a constitution upon an unwilling people, and nobody dreamed that any such attempt would be made, or deemed it necessary to provide for such a contingency. If such a clause was necessary in Mr. Trumbull's opinion, why did he not offer an amendment to that effect?

In order to give more pertinency to that question, I will read an extract from Trumbull's speech in the Senate, on the Toombs bill, made on the 2nd of July, 1856. He said:

"We are asked to amend this bill and make it perfect, and a liberal spirit seems to be manifested on the part of some senators to have a fair bill. It is difficult, I admit, to frame a bill that will give satisfaction to all, but to approach it, or come near it, I think two things must be done."

The first, then, he goes on to say, was the application of the Wilmot Proviso to the Territories, and the second the repeal of all the laws passed by the Territorial Legislature. He did not then say that it was necessary to put in a clause requiring the submission of the constitution. Why, if he thought such a provision necessary, did he not introduce it? He says in his speech that he was invited to offer amendments. Why did he not do so? He cannot pretend that he had no chance to do this, for he did offer some amendments, but none requiring submission.

I now proceed to show that Mr. Trumbull knew at the time that the bill was silent as to the subject of submission, and also that he, and everybody else, took it for granted that the constitution would be submitted. Now for the evidence. In his second speech he says: "The bill in many of its features meets my approbation." So he did not think it so very bad.

Further on he says:

"In regard to the measure introduced by the Senator from Georgia [Mr. Toombs], and recommended by the committee, I regard it, in many respects, as a most excellent bill; but we must look at it in the light of surrounding circumstances. In the condition of things now existing in the country, I do not consider it as a safe measure, nor one which will give peace; and I will give my reasons. First, it affords no immediate relief. It provides for taking a census of the voters in the Territory for an election in November, and the assembling of a convention in December, to form, if it thinks proper, a constitution for Kansas, preparatory to its admission into the Union as a State. It is not until December that the Convention is to meet. It would take some time to form a constitution. *I suppose that constitution would have to be ratified by the people before it becomes valid.*"

He there expressly declared that he supposed, under the bill, the constitution would have to be submitted to the people before it became valid. He went on to say:

"No provision is made in this bill for such a ratification. This is objectionable to my mind. I do not think the people should be bound by a constitution without passing upon it directly, themselves."

Why did he not offer an amendment providing for such a submission, if he thought it necessary? Notwithstanding the absence of such a clause he took it for granted that the constitution would have to be ratified by the people, under the bill.

In another part of the same speech, he says:

"There is nothing said in this bill, so far as I have discovered, about submitting the constitution which is to be framed to the people, for their sanction or rejection. Perhaps the Convention would have the right to submit it, if it should think proper; but it is certainly not compelled to do so, according to the provisions of the bill. If it is to be submitted to the people, it will take time, and it will not be until some time next year that this new constitution, affirmed and ratified by the people, would be submitted here to Congress for its acceptance; and what is to be the condition of that people in the meantime?"

You see that his argument then was that the Toombs bill would not get Kansas into the Union quick enough, and was objectionable on that account. He had no fears about this submission, or why did he not introduce an amendment to meet the case?

A voice: Why did n't you? You were chairman of the committee.

Mr. DOUGLAS: I will answer that question for you.

In the first place, no provision had ever before been put

in any similar act passed by Congress. I did not suppose that there was an honest man who would pretend that the omission of such a clause furnished evidence of a conspiracy or attempt to impose on the people. It could not be expected that such of us as did not think that omission was evidence of such a scheme would offer such an amendment; but if Trumbull then believed what he now says, why did he not offer the amendment, and try to prevent it, when he was, as he says, invited to do so?

In this connection I will tell you what the main point of discussion was: There was a bill pending to admit Kansas whenever she should have a population of 93,420, that being the ratio required for a member of Congress. Under that bill Kansas could not have become a State for some years, because she could not have had the requisite population. Mr. Toombs took it into his head to bring in a bill to admit Kansas then, with only twenty-five or thirty thousand people, and the question was whether we would allow Kansas to come in under this bill, or keep her out under mine until she had 93,420 people. The committee considered that question, and overruled me, by deciding in favor of the immediate admission of Kansas, and I reported accordingly. I hold in my hand a copy of the report which I made at that time. I will read from it: ·

"The point upon which your committee have entertained the most serious and grave doubts in regard to the propriety of indorsing the proposition relates to the fact that, in the absence of any census of the inhabitants, there is reason to apprehend that the Territory does not contain sufficient population to entitle them to demand admission under the treaty with France, if we take the ratio of representation for a member of Congress as the rule."

Thus you see that in the written report accompanying the bill, I said that the great difficulty with the committee was the question of population. In the same report I happened to refer to the question of submission. Now, listen to what I said about that:

"In the opinion of your committee, whenever a constitution shall be formed in any Territory, preparatory to its admission into the Union as a State, justice, the genius of our institutions, the whole theory of our republican system, imperatively demand that the voice of the people shall be fairly expressed, and their will embodied in that fundamental law, without fraud, or violence, or intimidation, or any other improper or unlawful influence, and subject to no other restrictions than those imposed by the Constitution of the United States."

I read this from the report I made at the time, on the Toombs bill. I will read yet another passage from the same report; after setting out the features of the Toombs bill, I contrast it with the proposition of Senator Seward, saying:

"The revised proposition of the Senator from Georgia refers all matters in dispute to the decision of the present population, with guarantees of fairness and safeguards against frauds and violence to which no reasonable man can find just grounds of exception; while the Senator from New York, if his proposition is designed to recognize and impart vitality to the Topeka Constitution, proposes to disfranchise, not only all the emigrants who have arrived in the Territory this year, but all the law-abiding men who refused to join in the act of open rebellion against the constituted authorities of the Territory last year, by making the unauthorized and unlawful action of a political party the fundamental law of the whole people."

Then, again, I repeat that under that bill the question is to be referred to the present population to decide for or against coming into the Union under the constitution they may adopt.

Mr. Trumbull, when at Chicago, rested his charge upon the allegation that the clause requiring submission was originally in the bill, and was stricken out by me. When that falsehood was exposed by a publication of the record, he went to Alton and made another speech, repeating the charge and referring to other and different evidence to sustain it. He saw that he was caught in his first falsehood, so he changed the issue, and instead of resting upon the allegation of striking out, he made it rest upon the declaration that I had introduced a clause into the bill prohibiting the people from voting upon the constitution. I am told that he made the same charge here that he made at Alton, that I had actually introduced and incorporated into the bill a clause which prohibited the people from voting upon their constitution. I hold his Alton speech in my hand, and will read the amendment which he alleges that I offered. It is in these words:

" And until the complete execution of this Act, no other election shall be held in said Territory."

Trumbull says the object of that amendment was to prevent the Convention from submitting the constitution to a vote of the people. I will read what he said at Alton on that subject:

" This clause put it out of the power of the Convention, had it been so disposed, to submit the constitution to the people for adoption; for it absolutely prohibited the holding of any other election than that for the election of delegates, till that Act was completely executed, which would not have been till Kansas was admitted as a State, or, at all events, till her constitution was fully prepared and ready for submission to Congress for admission."

Now, do you suppose that Mr. Trumbull supposed that that clause prohibited the Convention from submitting the constitution to the people, when, in his speech in the Senate, he declared that the Convention had a right to submit it? In his Alton speech, as will be seen by the extract which I have read, he declared the clause put it out of the power of the Convention to submit the constitution, and in his speech in the Senate he said:

"There is *nothing said in this bill*, so far as I have discovered, about submitting the constitution which is to be formed to the people, for their sanction or rejection. Perhaps the Convention would have the right to submit it, if it should think proper, but it is certainly not compelled to do so according to the provisions of the bill."

Thus you see that, in Congress, he declared the bill to be silent on the subject, and a few days since, at Alton, he made a speech and said that there was a provision in the bill prohibiting submission.

I have two answers to make to that. In the first place, the amendment which he quotes as depriving the people of an opportunity to vote upon the constitution *was stricken out on my motion*,—absolutely stricken out, and not voted on at all! In the second place, in lieu of it, a provision was voted in, authorizing the Convention to order an election whenever it pleased. I will read. After Trumbull had made his speech in the Senate, declaring that the constitution would probably be submitted to the people, although the bill was silent upon that subject, I made a few remarks, and offered two amendments, which you may find in the Appendix to the *Congressional Globe*, volume thirty-three, first session of the Thirty-fourth Congress, page 795. I quote:

"Mr. DOUGLAS: I have an amendment to offer from the Committee on Territories. On page 8, section 11, *strike out the words* 'until the complete execution of this act no other election shall be held in said Territory,' and insert the amendment which I hold in my hand."

The amendment was as follows:

"That all persons who shall possess the other qualifications prescribed for voters under this Act, and who shall have been *bona fide* inhabitants of said Territory since its organization, and who shall have absented themselves therefrom in consequence of the disturbances therein, and who shall return before the first day of October next, and become *bona fide* inhabitants of the Territory, with the intent of making it their permanent home, and shall present satisfactory evidence of these facts to the Board of Commissioners, shall be entitled to vote at said election, and shall have their names placed on said corrected list of voters for that purpose."

That amendment was adopted unanimously. After its adoption, the record shows the following:

"Mr. DOUGLAS: I have another amendment to offer from the Committee, to follow the one which has been adopted. The bill reads now, 'And until the complete execution of this Act, no other election shall be held in said Territory.' It has been suggested that it should be modified in this way, 'And to avoid all conflict in the complete execution of this Act, all other elections in said Territory are hereby postponed until such time as said Convention shall appoint,' so that they can appoint the day in the event that there should be a failure to come into the Union."

This amendment was also agreed to, without dissent.

Thus you see that the amendment quoted by Trumbull at Alton as evidence against me, instead of being put into the bill by me, was stricken out on my motion, and never became a part thereof at all. You also see that the substituted clause expressly authorized the Convention to appoint such day of election as it should deem proper.

Mr. Trumbull when he made that speech knew these facts. He forged his evidence from beginning to end, and by falsifying the record he endeavors to bolster up his false charge. I ask you what you think of Trumbull thus going around the country, falsifying and garbling the public records. I ask you whether you will sustain a man who will descend to the infamy of such conduct.

Mr. Douglas proceeded to remark that he should not hereafter occupy his time in refuting such charges made by Trumbull, but that, Lincoln having indorsed the character of Trumbull for veracity, he should hold him [Lincoln] responsible for the slanders.

FIFTH JOINT DEBATE, AT GALESBURGH,

OCTOBER 7, 1858.

MR. DOUGLAS'S SPEECH.

LADIES AND GENTLEMEN: Four years ago I appeared before the people of Knox County for the purpose of defending my political action upon the Compromise measures of 1850 and the passage of the Kansas-Nebraska Bill. Those of you before me who were present then will remember that I vindicated myself for supporting those two measures by the fact that they rested upon the great fundamental principle that the people of each State and each Territory of this Union have the right, and ought to be permitted to exercise the right, of regulating their own domestic concerns in their own way, subject to no other limitation or restriction than that which the Constitution of the United States imposes upon them. I then called upon the people of Illinois to decide whether that principle of self-government was right or wrong. If it was and is right, then the Compromise measures of 1850 were right, and consequently, the Kansas and Nebraska Bill, based upon the same principle, must necessarily have been right.

The Kansas and Nebraska Bill declared, in so many words, that it was the true intent and meaning of the act not to legislate slavery into any State or

Territory, nor to exclude it therefrom, but to leave the people thereof perfectly free to form and regulate their domestic institutions in their own way, subject only to the Constitution of the United States. For the last four years I have devoted all my energies, in private and public, to commend that principle to the American people. Whatever else may be said in condemnation or support of my political course I apprehend that no honest man will doubt the fidelity with which, under all circumstances, I have stood by it.

During the last year a question arose in the Congress of the United States whether or not that principle would be violated by the admission of Kansas into the Union under the Lecompton Constitution. In my opinion, the attempt to force Kansas in under that constitution was a gross violation of the principle enunciated in the Compromise measures of 1850, and Kansas and Nebraska Bill of 1854, and therefore I led off in the fight against the Lecompton Constitution, and conducted it until the effort to carry that constitution through Congress was abandoned. And I can appeal to all men, friends and foes, Democrats and Republicans, Northern men and Southern men, that during the whole of that fight I carried the banner of popular sovereignty aloft, and never allowed it to trail in the dust, or lowered my flag until victory perched upon our arms. When the Lecompton Constitution was defeated, the question arose in the minds of those who had advocated it what they should next resort to in order to carry out their views. They devised a measure known as the English bill, and granted a general amnesty and political pardon to all men who had fought against the Lecompton Constitution, provided they would support that bill. I for one did not choose to accept the pardon, or to avail myself of the amnesty granted on that condition. The fact that the supporters of Lecompton were willing to forgive all differences of opinion at that time in the event those who opposed it favored the English bill, was an admission they did not think that opposition to Lecompton impaired a man's standing in the Democratic party. Now, the question arises, what was that English bill which certain men are now attempting to make a test of political orthodoxy in this country? It provided, in substance, that the Lecompton Constitution should be sent back to the people of Kansas for their adoption or rejection, at an election which was held in August last, and in case they refused admission under it, that Kansas should be kept out of the Union until she had 93,420 inhabitants. I was in favor of sending the constitution back in order to enable the people to say whether or not it was their act and deed, and embodied their will; but the other proposition, that if they refused to come into the Union under it they should be kept out until they had double or treble the population they then had, I never would sanction by my vote. The reason why I could not sanction it is to be found in the fact that by the English bill, if the people of Kansas had only agreed to become a slaveholding State under the Lecompton Constitution, they could have done so with 35,000 people, but if they insisted on being a free State, as they had a right to do, then they were to be punished by being kept out of the Union until they had nearly three times that population. I then said in my place in the Senate, as I now say to you, that whenever Kansas has population enough for a slave State she has population enough for a free State. I have never yet given a vote, and I never intend to record one, making an odious and unjust distinction between the different States of this Union. I hold it to be a fundamental principle in our republican form of government that all the States of this Union, old and new, free and slave, stand on an exact equality. Equality among the different States is a cardinal principle on which all our institutions rest. Wherever, therefore, you make a discrimination, saving to a slave State that it shall be admitted with 35,000 inhabitants, and a free State that it shall not be admitted until it has 93,000 or 100,000 inhabitants, you are throwing the whole weight of the Federal Government into the scale in favor of one class of States against the other. Nor would I, on the other hand, any sooner sanction the doctrine that a free State could be admitted into the Union with 35,000 people, while a slave State was kept out until it had 93,000. I have always declared in the Senate my willingness, and I am willing now to adopt the rule, that no Territory shall ever become a State until it has the requisite population for a member of Congress, according to the then existing ratio. But while I have always been, and am now, willing to adopt that general rule, I was not willing and would not consent to make an exception of Kansas, as a punishment for her obstinacy in demanding the right to do as she pleased in the formation of her constitution. It is proper that I should remark here, that my opposition to the Lecompton Constitution did not rest upon the peculiar position taken by Kansas on the subject of slavery. I held then, and hold now, that if the people of Kansas want a slave State, it is their right to make one, and be received into the Union under it; if, on the contrary, they want a free State, it is their right to have it, and no man should ever oppose their admission because they ask it under the one or the other. I hold to that great principle of self-government which asserts the right of every people to decide for themselves the nature and character of the domestic institutions and fundamental law under which they are to live.

The effort has been and is now being made in this State by certain postmasters and other Federal office-holders to make a test of faith on the support of the English bill. These men are now making speeches all over the State against me and in favor of Lincoln, either directly or indirectly, because I would not sanction a discrimination between slave and free States by voting for the English bill. But while that bill is made a test in Illinois for the purpose of breaking up the Democratic organization in this State, how is it in the other States? Go to Indiana, and there you find English himself, the author of the English bill, who is a candidate for re-election to Congress, has been forced by public opinion to

abandon his own darling project, and to give a
promise that he will vote for the admission of
Kansas at once, whenever she forms a constitution
in pursuance of law and ratifies it by a majority
vote of her people.   Not only is this the case with
English himself, but I am informed that every
Democratic candidate for Congress in Indiana takes
the same ground.   Pass to Ohio, and there you find
that Groesbeck, and Pendleton, and Cox, and all the
other anti-Lecompton men who stood shoulder to
shoulder with me against the Lecompton Constitution, but voted for the English bill, now repudiate it
and take the same ground that I do on that question.
So it is with the Joneses and others of Pennsylvania,
and so it is with every other Lecompton Democrat
in the free States.   They now abandon even the
English bill, and come back to the true platform
which I proclaimed at the time in the Senate, and
upon which the Democracy of Illinois now stand.
And yet, notwithstanding the fact that every Lecompton and anti-Lecompton Democrat in the free
States has abandoned the English bill, you are told
that it is to be made a test upon me, while the power
and patronage of the Government are all exerted to
elect men to Congress in the other States who occupy
the same position with reference to it that I do.   It
seems that my political offence consists in the fact
that I first did not vote for the English bill, and
thus pledge myself to keep Kansas out of the Union
until she has a population of 93,420, and then return home, violate that pledge, repudiate the bill,
and take the opposite ground.   If I had done this,

7

perhaps the Administration would now be advocating
my re-election, as it is that of the others who have
pursued this course. I did not choose to give that
pledge, for the reason that I did not intend to carry
out that principle. I never will consent, for the
sake of conciliating the frowns of power, to pledge
myself to do that which I do not intend to perform.
I now submit the question to you, as my constituency, whether I was not right, first, in resisting
the adoption of the Lecompton Constitution, and,
secondly, in resisting the English bill. I repeat that
I opposed the Lecompton Constitution because it
was not the act and deed of the people of Kansas,
and did not embody their will. I denied the right
of any power on earth, under our system of government, to force a constitution on an unwilling people.
There was a time when some men could pretend to
believe that the Lecompton Constitution embodied
the will of the people of Kansas; but that time has
passed. The question was referred to the people of
Kansas under the English bill last August, and then,
at a fair election, they rejected the Lecompton Constitution by a vote of from eight to ten against it to
one in its favor. Since it has been voted down by
so overwhelming a majority, no man can pretend
that it was the act and deed of that people. I submit the question to you whether or not, if it had not
been for me, that constitution would have been
crammed down the throats of the people of Kansas
against their consent. While at least ninety-nine
out of every hundred people here present agree that I
was right in defeating that project, yet my enemies

use the fact that I did defeat it, by doing right, to break me down and put another man in the United States Senate in my place. The very men who acknowledge that I was right in defeating Lecompton now form an alliance with Federal office-holders, professed Lecompton men, to defeat me, because I did right. My political opponent, Mr. Lincoln, has no hope on earth, and has never dreamed that he had a chance of success, were it not for the aid that he is receiving from Federal office-holders, who are using their influence and the patronage of the government against me in revenge for my having defeated the Lecompton Constitution. What do you Republicans think of a political organization that will try to make an unholy and unnatural combination with its professed foes to beat a man merely because he has done right? You know such is the fact with regard to your own party. You know that the axe of decapitation is suspended over every man in office in Illinois, and the terror of proscription is threatened every Democrat by the present Administration, unless he supports the Republican ticket in preference to my Democratic associates and myself. I could find an instance in the postmaster of the city of Galesburgh, and in every other postmaster in this vicinity, all of whom have been stricken down simply because they discharged the duties of their offices honestly, and supported the regular Democratic ticket in this State in the right. The Republican party is availing itself of unworthy means in the present contest to carry the election, because its leaders know that if they let this chance slip they will never have another, and their hopes of making this a Republican State will be blasted forever.

Now, let me ask you whether the country has any interest in sustaining this organization, known as the Republican party. That party is unlike all other political organizations in this country. All other parties have been national in their character,— have avowed their principles alike in the slave and free States, in Kentucky as well as Illinois, in Louisiana as well as in Massachusetts. Such was the case with the old Whig party, and such was and is the case with the Democratic party. Whigs and Democrats could proclaim their principles boldly and fearlessly in the North and in the South, in the East and in the West, wherever the Constitution ruled, and the American flag waved over American soil.

But now you have a sectional organization, a party which appeals to the Northern section of the Union against the Southern, a party which appeals to Northern passion, Northern pride, Northern ambition, and Northern prejudices, against Southern people, the Southern States, and Southern institutions. The leaders of that party hope that they will be able to unite the Northern States in one great sectional party; and inasmuch as the North is the strongest section, that they will thus be enabled to outvote, conquer, govern and control the South. Hence you find that they now make speeches advocating principles and measures which cannot be defended in any slaveholding State of this Union. Is there a Republican residing in Galesburgh who can travel into Kentucky and carry his principles with

him across the Ohio? What Republican from
Massachusetts can visit the Old Dominion without
leaving his principles behind him when he crosses
Mason and Dixon's line? Permit me to say to you
in perfect good-humor, but in all sincerity, that no
political creed is sound which cannot be proclaimed
fearlessly in every State of this Union where the
Federal Constitution is the supreme law of the land.
Not only is this Republican party unable to proclaim its principles alike in the North and South, in
the free States and in the slave States, but it cannot
even proclaim them in the same forms and give them
the same strength and meaning in all parts of the
same State. My friend Lincoln finds it extremely
difficult to manage a debate in the centre part of the
State, where there is a mixture of men from the
North and the South. In the extreme northern part
of Illinois he can proclaim as bold and radical Abolitionism as ever Giddings, Lovejoy, or Garrison
enunciated; but when he gets down a little farther
south he claims that he is an old-line Whig, a dis-
ciple of Henry Clay, and declares that he still
adheres to the old-line Whig creed, and has nothing
whatever to do with Abolitionism, or negro equality,
or negro citizenship. I once before hinted this of
Mr. Lincoln in a public speech, and at Charleston he
defied me to show that there was any difference
between his speeches in the North and in the South,
and that they were not in strict harmony. I will
now call your attention to two of them, and you can
then say whether you would be apt to believe that
the same man ever uttered both. In a speech in

reply to me at Chicago in July last, Mr. Lincoln, in speaking of the equality of the negro with the white man, used the following language:

"I should like to know, if, taking this old Declaration of Independence, which declares that all men are equal upon principle, and making exceptions to it, where will it stop? If one man says it does not mean a negro, why may not another man say it does not mean another man? If the Declaration is not the truth, let us get the statute book in which we find it, and tear it out. Who is so bold as to do it? If it is not true, let us tear it out."

You find that Mr. Lincoln there proposed that if the doctrine of the Declaration of Independence, declaring all men to be born equal, did not include the negro and put him on an equality with the white man, that we should take the statute book and tear it out. He there took the ground that the negro race is included in the Declaration of Independence as the equal of the white race, and that there could be no such thing as a distinction in the races, making one superior and the other inferior. I read now from the same speech:

"My friends [he says], I have detained you about as long as I desire to do, and I have only to say, let us discard all this quibbling about this man and the other man, this race and that race and the other race being inferior, and therefore they must be placed in an inferior position, discarding our standard that we have left us. Let us discard all these things, and unite as one people throughout this land, until we shall once more stand up declaring that all men are created equal."

["That's right," etc.]

Yes, I have no doubt that you think it is right; but the Lincoln men down in Coles, Tazewell, and Sangamon counties *do not* think it is right. In the conclusion of the same speech, talking to the Chicago Abolitionists, he said : "I leave you, hoping that the lamp of liberty will burn in your bosoms until there shall no longer be a doubt that all men are created free and equal." [["Good, good."] Well, you say "Good " to that, and you are going to vote for Lincoln because he holds that doctrine. I will not blame you for supporting him on that ground, but I will show you, in immediate contrast with that doctrine, what Mr. Lincoln said down in Egypt in order to get votes in that locality, where they do not hold to such a doctrine. In a joint discussion between Mr. Lincoln and myself, at Charleston, I think, on the 18th of last month, Mr. Lincoln, referring to this subject, used the following language:

"I will say then, that I am not, nor never have been, in favor of bringing about in any way the social and political equality of the white and black races; that I am not, nor ever have been, in favor of making voters of the free negroes, or jurors, or qualifying them to hold office, or having them to marry with white people. I will say, in addition, that there is a physical difference between the white and black races which, I suppose, will forever forbid the two races living together upon terms of social and political equality; and inasmuch as they cannot so live, that while they do remain together there must be the position of superior and inferior, that I as much as any other man am in favor of the superior position being assigned to the white man."

["Good for Lincoln."]

Fellow-citizens, here you find men hurrahing for Lincoln, and saying that he did right, when in one part of the State he stood up for negro equality, and in another part, for political effect, discarded the doctrine, and declared that there always must be a superior and inferior race. Abolitionists up North are expected and required to vote for Lincoln because he goes for the equality of the races, holding that by the Declaration of Independence the white man and the negro were created equal, and endowed by the divine law with that equality, and down South he tells the old Whigs, the Kentuckians, Virginians, and Tennesseeans, that there is a physical difference in the races, making one superior and the other inferior, and that he is in favor of maintaining the superiority of the white race over the negro. Now, how can you reconcile those two positions of Mr. Lincoln? He is to be voted for in the South as a pro-slavery man, and he is to be voted for in the North as an Abolitionist. Up here he thinks it is all nonsense to talk about a difference between the races, and says that we must "discard all quibbling about this race and that race and the other race being inferior, and therefore they must be placed in an inferior position." Down South he makes this "quibble" about this race and that race and the other race being inferior as the creed of his party, and declares that the negro can never be elevated to the position of the white man. You find that his political meetings are called by different names in different counties in the State. Here they are called

Republican meetings; but in old Tazewell, where Lincoln made a speech last Tuesday, he did not address a *Republican* meeting, but "a grand rally of the *Lincoln men*." There are very few Republicans there, because Tazewell County is filled with old Virginians and Kentuckians, all of whom are Whigs or Democrats; and if Mr. Lincoln had called an Abolition or Republican meeting there, he would not get many votes. Go down into Egypt, and you will find that he and his party are operating under an alias there, which his friend Trumbull has given them, in order that they may cheat the people. When I was down in Monroe County a few weeks ago, addressing the people, I saw handbills posted announcing that Mr. Trumbull was going to speak in behalf of Lincoln; and what do you think the name of his party was there? Why, the "*Free Democracy*." Mr. Trumbull and Mr. Jehu Baker were announced to address the Free Democracy of Monroe County, and the bill was signed, "Many Free Democrats." The reason that Lincoln and his party adopted the name of "Free Democracy" down there was because Monroe County has always been an old-fashioned Democratic county, and hence it was necessary to make the people believe that they were Democrats, sympathized with them, and were fighting for Lincoln as Democrats. Come up to Springfield, where Lincoln now lives, and always has lived, and you find that the Convention of his party which assembled to nominate candidates for Legislature, who are expected to vote for him if elected, dare not adopt the name of Republican, but assembled under

the title of "all opposed to the Democracy." Thus
you find that Mr. Lincoln's creed cannot travel
through even one half of the counties of this State,
but that it changes its hues and becomes lighter and
lighter as it travels from the extreme north, until
it is nearly white when it reaches the extreme south
end of the State.

I ask you, my friends, why cannot Republicans
avow their principles alike everywhere? I would
despise myself if I thought that I was procuring
your votes by concealing my opinions, and by avow-
ing one set of principles in one part of the State, and
a different set in another part. If I do not truly
and honorably represent your feelings and principles,
then I ought not to be your Senator; and I will never
conceal my opinions, or modify or change them a
hair's breadth, in order to get votes. I tell you that
this Chicago doctrine of Lincoln's—declaring that the
negro and the white man are made equal by the
Declaration of Independence and by Divine Providence—is a monstrous heresy. The signers of the
Declaration of Independence never dreamed of the
negro when they were writing that document. They
referred to white men, to men of European birth,
and European descent, when they declared the
equality of all men. I see a gentleman there in the
crowd shaking his head. Let me remind him that
when Thomas Jefferson wrote that document, he was
the owner, and so continued until his death, of a large
number of slaves. Did he intend to say in that
Declaration that his negro slaves, which he held and
treated as property, were created his equals by

divine law, and that he was violating the law of God every day of his life by holding them as slaves? It must be borne in mind that when that Declaration was put forth, every one of the thirteen Colonies were slaveholding Colonies, and every man who signed that instrument represented a slaveholding constituency. Recollect, also, that no one of them emancipated his slaves, much less put them on an equality with himself, after he signed the Declaration. On the contrary, they all continued to hold their negroes as slaves during the Revolutionary War. Now, do you believe—are you willing to have it said —that every man who signed the Declaration of Independence declared the negro his equal, and then was hypocrite enough to continue to hold him as a slave, in violation of what he believed to be the divine law? And yet when you say that the Declaration of Independence includes the negro, you charge the signers of it with hypocrisy.

I say to you, frankly, that in my opinion this government was made by our fathers on the white basis. It was made by white men for the benefit of white men and their posterity forever, and was intended to be administered by white men in all time to come. But while I hold that under our Constitution and political system the negro is not a citizen, cannot be a citizen, and ought not to be a citizen, it does not follow by any means that he should be a slave. On the contrary, it does follow that the negro, as an inferior race, ought to possess every right, every privilege, every immunity, which he can safely exercise, consistent with the safety of the society in which he lives. Humanity requires, and Christianity commands, that you shall extend to every inferior being, and every dependent being, all the privileges, immunities, and advantages which can be granted to them, consistent with the safety of society. If you ask me the nature and extent of these privileges, I answer that that is a question which the people of each State must decide for themselves. Illinois has decided that question for herself. We have said that in this State the negro shall not be a slave, nor shall he be a citizen. Kentucky holds a different doctrine. New York holds one different from either, and Maine one different from all. Virginia, in her policy on this question, differs in many respects from the others, and so on, until there are hardly two States whose policy is exactly alike in regard to the relation of the white man and the negro. Nor can you reconcile them and make them alike. Each State must do as it pleases. Illinois had as much right to adopt the policy which we have on that subject as Kentucky had to adopt a different policy. The great principle of this government is, that each State has the right to do as it pleases on all these questions, and no other State or power on earth has the right to interfere with us, or complain of us merely because our system differs from theirs. In the Compromise measures of 1850, Mr. Clay declared that this great principle ought to exist in the Territories as well as in the States, and I reasserted his doctrine in the Kansas and Nebraska Bill of 1854.

But Mr. Lincoln cannot be made to understand,

and those who are determined to vote for him, no matter whether he is a pro-slavery man in the South and a negro equality advocate in the North, cannot be made to understand how it is that in a Territory the people can do as they please on the slavery question under the Dred Scott decision. Let us see whether I cannot explain it to the satisfaction of all impartial men. Chief Justice Taney has said, in his opinion in the Dred Scott case, that a negro slave, being property, stands on an equal footing with other property, and that the owner may carry them into United States territory the same as he does other property. Suppose any two of you, neighbors, should conclude to go to Kansas, one carrying $100,000 worth of negro slaves, and the other $100,000 worth of mixed merchandise, including quantities of liquors. You both agree that under that decision you may carry your property to Kansas; but when you get it there, the merchant who is possessed of the liquors is met by the Maine liquor law, which prohibits the sale or use of his property, and the owner of the slaves is met by equally unfriendly legislation, which makes his property worthless after he gets it there. What is the right to carry your property into the Territory worth to either, when unfriendly legislation in the Territory renders it worthless after you get it there? The slaveholder when he gets his slaves there finds that there is no local law to protect him in holding them, no slave code, no police regulation maintaining and supporting him in his right, and he discovers at once that the absence of such friendly legislation

excludes his property from the Territory just as ir-
resistibly as if there was a positive constitutional
prohibition excluding it.   Thus you find it is with
any kind of property in a Territory: it depends for
its protection on the local and municipal law.   If
the people of a Territory want slavery, they make
friendly legislation to introduce it; but if they do
not want it, they withhold all protection from it,
and then it cannot exist there.   Such was the view
taken on the subject by different Southern men when
the Nebraska Bill passed.   See the speech of Mr. Orr,
of South Carolina, the present Speaker of the House
of Representatives of Congress, made at that time;
and there you will find this whole doctrine argued
out at full length.   Read the speeches of other
Southern Congressmen, Senators and Representatives, made in 1854, and you will find that they took
the same view of the subject as Mr. Orr,—that
slavery could never be forced on a people who did not
want it.   I hold that in this country there is no
power on the face of the globe that can force any
institution on an unwilling people.   The great fundamental principle of our government is that the people
of each State and each Territory shall be left perfectly free to decide for themselves what shall be the
nature and character of their institutions.   When
this government was made, it was based on that
principle.   At the time of its formation there were
twelve slaveholding States and one free State in this
Union.   Suppose this doctrine of Mr. Lincoln and
the Republicans, of uniformity of laws of all the
States on the subject of slavery, had prevailed; sup-

pose Mr. Lincoln himself had been a member of the Convention which framed the Constitution, and that he had risen in that august body, and, addressing the father of his country, had said as he did at Springfield: "A house divided against itself cannot stand. I believe this government cannot endure permanently, half slave and half free. I do not expect the Union to be dissolved, I do not expect the house to fall, but I do expect it will cease to be divided. It will become all one thing or all the other." What do you think would have been the result? Suppose he had made that Convention believe that doctrine, and they had acted upon it, what do you think would have been the result? Do you believe that the one free State would have outvoted the twelve slaveholding States, and thus abolish slavery? On the contrary, would not the twelve slaveholding States have outvoted the one free State, and under his doctrine have fastened slavery by an irrevocable constitutional provision upon every inch of the American Republic? Thus you see that the doctrine he now advocates, if proclaimed at the beginning of the government, would have established slavery everywhere throughout the American continent; and are you willing, now that we have the majority section, to exercise a power which we never would have submitted to when we were in the minority? If the Southern States had attempted to control our institutions, and make the States all slave, when they had the power, I ask would you have submitted to it? If you would not, are you willing, now that we have become the strongest, under that great principle of self-government that allows each State to do as it pleases, to attempt to control the Southern institutions?   Then, my friends, I say to you that there is but one path of peace in this Republic, and that is to administer this government as our fathers made it, divided into free and slave States, allowing each State to decide for itself whether it wants slavery or not.   If Illinois will settle the slavery question for herself, and mind her own business and let her neighbors alone, we will be at peace with Kentucky and every other Southern State.   If every other State in the Union will do the same, there will be peace between the North and the South, and in the whole Union.

MR. LINCOLN'S REPLY.

MY FELLOW-CITIZENS: A very large portion of the speech which Judge Douglas has addressed to you has previously been delivered and put in print.   I do not mean that for a hit upon the Judge at all. If I had not been interrupted, I was going to say that such an answer as I was able to make to a very large portion of it had already been more than once made and published.   There has been an opportunity afforded to the public to see our respective views upon the topics discussed in a large portion of the speech which he has just delivered.   I make these remarks for the purpose of excusing myself for not passing over the entire ground that the Judge has traversed.   I however desire to take up some of the points that he has attended to, and ask your attention to them, and I shall follow him backwards upon some notes which I have taken, reversing the order, by beginning where he concluded.

The Judge has alluded to the Declaration of Independence, and insisted that negroes are not included in that Declaration; and that it is a slander upon the framers of that instrument to suppose that negroes were meant therein; and he asks you: Is it possible to believe that Mr. Jefferson, who penned the immortal paper, could have supposed himself applying the language of that instrument to the negro race, and yet held a portion of that race in slavery? Would he not at once have freed them? I only have to remark upon this part of the Judge's speech (and that, too, very briefly, for I shall not detain myself, or you, upon that point for any great length of time), that I believe the entire records of the world, from the date of the Declaration of Independence up to within three years ago, may be searched in vain for one single affirmation, from one single man, that the negro was not included in the Declaration of Independence; I think I may defy Judge Douglas to show that he ever said so, that Washington ever said so, that any President ever said so, that any member of Congress ever said so, or that any living man upon the whole earth ever said so, until the necessities of the present policy of the Democratic party, in regard to slavery, had to invent that affirmation. And I will remind Judge Douglas and this audience that while Mr. Jefferson was the owner of slaves, as undoubtedly he was, in speaking upon this very subject he used the strong language that "he trembled

8

for his country when he remembered that God was just"; and I will offer the highest premium in my power to Judge Douglas if he will show that he, in all his life, ever uttered a sentiment at all akin to that of Jefferson.

The next thing to which I will ask your attention is the Judge's comments upon the fact, as he assumes it to be, that we cannot call our public meetings as Republican meetings; and he instances Tazewell County as one of the places where the friends of Lincoln have called a public meeting and have not dared to name it a Republican meeting. He instances Monroe County as another, where Judge Trumbull and Jehu Baker addressed the persons whom the Judge assumes to be the friends of Lincoln, calling them the "Free Democracy." I have the honor to inform Judge Douglas that he spoke in that very county of Tazewell last Saturday, and I was there on Tuesday last; and when he spoke there, he spoke under a call not venturing to use the word "Democrat." [Turning to Judge Douglas.] What think you of this?

So, again, there is another thing to which I would ask the Judge's attention upon this subject. In the contest of 1856 his party delighted to call themselves together as the "National Democracy"; but now, if there should be a notice put up anywhere for a meeting of the "National Democracy," Judge Douglas and his friends would not come. They would not suppose themselves invited. They would understand that it was a call for those hateful postmasters whom he talks about.

Now a few words in regard to these extracts from speeches of mine which Judge Douglas has read to you, and which he supposes are in very great contrast to each other. Those speeches have been before the public for a considerable time, and if they have any inconsistency in them, if there is any conflict in them, the public have been able to detect it. When the Judge says, in speaking on this subject, that I make speeches of one sort for the people of the northern end of the State, and of a different sort for the southern people, he assumes that I do not understand that my speeches will be put in print and read north and south. I knew all the while that the speech that I made at Chicago, and the one I made at Jonesboro and the one at Charleston, would all be put in print, and all the reading and intelligent men in the community would see them and know all about my opinions. And I have not supposed, and do not now suppose, that there is any conflict whatever between them. But the Judge will have it that if we do not confess that there is a sort of inequality between the white and black races which justifies us in making them slaves, we must then insist that there is a degree of equality that requires us to make them our wives. Now, I have all the while taken a broad distinction in regard to that matter; and that is all there is in these different speeches which he arrays here; and the entire reading of either of the speeches will show that that distinction was made. Perhaps by taking two parts of the same speech he could have got up as much of a conflict as the one he has found. I have all the while maintained that in so far as it should be insisted that there was an equality between the white and black races that should produce a perfect social and political equality, it was an impossibility. This you have seen in my printed speeches, and with it I have said that in their right to "life, liberty, and the pursuit of happiness," as proclaimed in that old Declaration, the inferior races are our equals. And these declarations I have constantly made in reference to the abstract moral question, to contemplate and consider when we are legislating about any new country which is not already cursed with the actual presence of the evil,—slavery. I have never manifested any impatience with the necessities that spring from the actual presence of black people amongst us, and the actual existence of slavery amongst us where it does already exist; but I have insisted that, in legislating for new countries where it does not exist there is no just rule other than that of moral and abstract right! With reference to those new countries, those maxims as to the right of a people to "life, liberty, and the pursuit of happiness" were the just rules to be constantly referred to. There is no misunderstanding this, except by men interested to misunderstand it. I take it that I have to address an intelligent and reading community, who will peruse what I say, weigh it, and then judge whether I advanced improper or unsound views, or whether I advanced hypocritical, and deceptive, and contrary views in different portions of the country. I believe myself to be guilty of no such thing as the latter, though, of course, I cannot claim that I am entirely free from all error in the opinions I advance.

The Judge has also detained us awhile in regard to the distinction between his party and our party. His he assumes to be a national party,—ours a sectional one. He does this in asking the question whether this country has any interest in the maintenance of the Republican party. He assumes that our party is altogether sectional, that the party to which he adheres is national; and the argument is, that no party can be a rightful party—can be based upon rightful principles—unless it can announce its principles everywhere. I presume that Judge Douglas could not go into Russia and announce the doctrine of our national Democracy; he could not denounce the doctrine of kings and emperors and monarchies in Russia; and it may be true of this country that in some places we may not be able to proclaim a doctrine as clearly true as the truth of democracy, because there is a section so directly opposed to it that they will not tolerate us in doing so. Is it the true test of the soundness of a doctrine that in some places people won't let you proclaim it? Is that the way to test the truth of any doctrine? Why, I understood that at one time the people of Chicago would not let Judge Douglas preach a certain favorite doctrine of his. I commend to his consideration the question whether he takes that as a test of the unsoundness of what he wanted to preach.

There is another thing to which I wish to ask attention for a little while on this occasion. What has always been the evidence brought forward to prove that the Republican party is a sectional party? The main one was that in the Southern portion of the

Union the people did not let the Republicans proclaim their doctrines amongst them. That has been the main evidence brought forward,—that they had no supporters, or substantially none, in the Slave States. The South have not taken hold of our principles as we announce them; nor does Judge Douglas now grapple with those principles. We have a Republican State Platform, laid down in Springfield in June last, stating our position all the way through the questions before the country. We are now far advanced in this canvass. Judge Douglas and I have made perhaps forty speeches apiece, and we have now for the fifth time met face to face in debate, and up to this day I have not found either Judge Douglas or any friend of his taking hold of the Republican platform, or laying his finger upon anything in it that is wrong. I ask you all to recollect that. Judge Douglas turns away from the platform of principles to the fact that he can find people somewhere who will not allow us to announce those principles. If he had great confidence that our principles were wrong, he would take hold of them and demonstrate them to be wrong. But he does not do so. The only evidence he has of their being wrong is in the fact that there are people who won't allow us to preach them. I ask again, is that the way to test the soundness of a doctrine?

I ask his attention also to the fact that by the rule of nationality he is himself fast becoming sectional. I ask his attention to the fact that his speeches would not go as current now south of the Ohio River as they have formerly gone there. I ask his attention to the fact that he felicitates himself to-day that all the Democrats of the free States are agreeing with him, while he omits to tell us that the Democrats of any slave State agree with him. If he has not thought of this, I commend to his consideration the evidence in his own declaration, on this day, of his becoming sectional too. I see it rapidly approaching. Whatever may be the result of this ephemeral contest between Judge Douglas and myself, I see the day rapidly approaching when his pill of sectionalism, which he has been thrusting down the throats of Republicans for years past, will be crowded down his own throat.

Now, in regard to what Judge Douglas said (in the beginning of his speech) about the Compromise of 1850 containing the principles of the Nebraska Bill, although I have often presented my views upon that subject, yet as I have not done so in this canvass, I will, if you please, detain you a little with them. I have always maintained, so far as I was able, that there was nothing of the principle of the Nebraska Bill in the Compromise of 1850 at all,—nothing whatever. Where can you find the principle of the Nebraska Bill in that Compromise? If anywhere, in the two pieces of the Compromise organizing the Territories of New Mexico and Utah. It was expressly provided in these two acts that when they came to be admitted into the Union they should be admitted with or without slavery, as they should choose, by their own constitutions. Nothing was said in either of those acts as to what was to be done in relation to slavery during the Territorial existence of those Territories, while Henry Clay constantly made the declaration (Judge Douglas recognizing him as a leader) that, in his opinion, the old Mexican laws would control that question during the Territorial existence, and that these old Mexican laws excluded slavery. How can that be used as a principle for declaring that during the Territorial existence as well as at the time of framing the constitution the people, if you please, might have slaves if they wanted them? I am not discussing the question whether it is right or wrong; but how are the New Mexican and Utah laws patterns for the Nebraska Bill? I maintain that the organization of Utah and New Mexico *did not* establish a general principle at all. It had no feature of establishing a general principle. The acts to which I have referred were a part of a general system of Compromises. They did not lay down what was proposed as a regular policy for the Territories, only an agreement in this particular case to do in that way, because other things were done that were to be a compensation for it. They were allowed to come in in that shape, because in another way it was paid for,—considering that as a part of that system of measures called the Compromise of 1850, which finally included half-a-dozen acts. It included the admission of California as a free State, which was kept out of the Union for half a year because it had formed a free constitution. It included the settlement of the boundary of Texas, which had been undefined before, which was in itself a slavery question; for if you pushed the line farther west, you made Texas larger, and made more slave territory; while, if you drew the line toward the east, you narrowed the boundary and diminished the domain of slavery, and by so much increased free territory. It included the abolition of the slave trade in the District of Columbia. It included the passage of a new Fugitive Slave law. All these things were put together, and, though passed in separate acts, were nevertheless, in legislation (as the speeches at the time will show), made to depend upon each other. Each got votes with the understanding that the other measures were to pass, and by this system of compromise, in that series of measures, those two bills—the New Mexico and Utah bills —were passed: and I say for that reason they could not be taken as models, framed upon their own intrinsic principle, for all future Territories. And I have the evidence of this in the fact that Judge Douglas, a year afterward, or more than a year afterward, perhaps, when he first introduced bills for the purpose of framing new Territories, did not attempt to follow these bills of New Mexico and Utah; and even when he introduced this Nebraska Bill, I think you will discover that he did not exactly follow them. But I do not wish to dwell at great length upon this branch of the discussion. My own opinion is, that a thorough investigation will show most plainly that the New Mexico and Utah bills were part of a system of compromise, and not designed as patterns for future Territorial legislation; and that this Nebraska Bill did not follow them as a pattern at all.

The Judge tells, in proceeding, that he is opposed to making any odious distinctions between free and

slave States. I am altogether unaware that the
Republicans are in favor of making any odious distinctions between the free and slave States. But
there is still a difference, I think, between Judge
Douglas and the Republicans in this. I suppose that
the real difference between Judge Douglas and his
friends, and the Republicans on the contrary, is,
that the Judge is not in favor of making any difference between slavery and liberty; that he is in favor
of eradicating, of pressing out of view, the questions
of preference in this country for free or slave institutions; and consequently every sentiment he utters
discards the idea that there is any wrong in slavery.
Everything that emanates from him or his coadjutors
in their course of policy carefully excludes the thought
that there is anything wrong in slavery. All their
arguments, if you will consider them, will be seen to
exclude the thought that there is anything whatever
wrong in slavery. If you will take the Judge's
speeches, and select the short and pointed sentences
expressed by him,—as his declaration that he "don't
care whether slavery is voted up or down,"—you will
see at once that this is perfectly logical, if you do not
admit that slavery is wrong. If you do admit that it
is wrong, Judge Douglas cannot logically say he don't
care whether a wrong is voted up or voted down.
Judge Douglas declares that if any community wants
slavery they have a right to have it. He can say
that logically, if he says that there is no wrong in
slavery; but if you admit that there is a wrong in it,
he cannot logically say that anybody has a right to
do wrong. He insists that upon the score of equality

the owners of slaves and owners of property—of
horses and every other sort of property—should be
alike, and hold them alike in a new Territory. That
is perfectly logical if the two species of property are
alike and are equally founded in right. But if you
admit that one of them is wrong, you cannot institute any equality between right and wrong. And
from this difference of sentiment,—the belief on the
part of one that the institution is wrong, and a policy
springing from that belief which looks to the arrest
of the enlargement of that wrong, and this other
sentiment, that it is no wrong, and a policy sprung
from that sentiment, which will tolerate no idea of
preventing the wrong from growing larger, and looks
to there never being an end to it through all the existence of things,—arises the real difference between
Judge Douglas and his friends on the one hand and
the Republicans on the other. Now, I confess myself as belonging to that class in the country who
contemplate slavery as a moral, social, and political
evil, having due regard for its actual existence
amongst us and the difficulties of getting rid of it in
any satisfactory way, and to all the constitutional
obligations which have been thrown about it; but,
nevertheless, desire a policy that looks to the pre-
vention of it as a wrong, and looks hopefully to the
time when as a wrong it may come to an end.

Judge Douglas has again, for, I believe, the fifth
time, if not the seventh, in my presence, reiterated
his charge of a conspiracy or combination between
the National Democrats and Republicans. What
evidence Judge Douglas has upon this subject I

know not, inasmuch as he never favors us with any. I have said upon a former occasion, and I do not choose to suppress it now, that I have no objection to the division in the Judge's party. He got it up himself. It was all his and their work. He had, I think, a great deal more to do with the steps that led to the Lecompton Constitution than Mr. Buchanan had; though at last, when they reached it, they quarrelled over it, and their friends divided upon it. I am very free to confess to Judge Douglas that I have no objection to the division; but I defy the Judge to show any evidence that I have in any way promoted that division, unless he insists on being a witness himself in merely saying so. I can give all fair friends of Judge Douglas here to understand exactly the view that Republicans take in regard to that division. Don't you remember how two years ago the opponents of the Democratic party were divided between Fremont and Fillmore? I guess you do. Any Democrat who remembers that division will remember also that he was at the time very glad of it, and then he will be able to see all there is between the National Democrats and the Republicans. What we now think of the two divisions of Democrats, you then thought of the Fremont and Fillmore divisions. That is all there is of it.

But if the Judge continues to put forward the declaration that there is an unholy and unnatural alliance between the Republicans and the National Democrats, I now want to enter my protest against receiving him as an entirely competent witness upon that subject. I want to call to the Judge's attention an attack he made upon me in the first one of these debates, at Ottawa, on the 21st of August. In order to fix extreme Abolitionism upon me, Judge Douglas read a set of resolutions which he declared had been passed by a Republican State Convention, in October, 1854, at Springfield, Illinois, and he declared I had taken part in that Convention. It turned out that although a few men calling themselves an anti-Nebraska State Convention had sat at Springfield about that time, yet neither did I take any part in it, nor did it pass the resolutions or any such resolutions as Judge Douglas read. So apparent had it become that the resolutions which he read had not been passed at Springfield at all, nor by a State Convention in which I had taken part, that seven days afterward, at Freeport, Judge Douglas declared that he had been misled by Charles H. Lanphier, editor of the *State Register*, and Thomas L. Harris, member of Congress in that district, and he promised in that speech that when he went to Springfield he would investigate the matter. Since then Judge Douglas has been to Springfield, and I presume has made the investigation; but a month has passed since he has been there, and, so far as I know, he has made no report of the result of his investigation. I have waited as I think sufficient time for the report of that investigation, and I have some curiosity to see and hear it. A fraud, an absolute forgery was committed, and the perpetration of it was traced to the three, — Lanphier, Harris, and Douglas. Whether it can be narrowed in any way so as to exonerate any one of them, is what Judge Douglas's report would probably show.

It is true that the set of resolutions read by Judge Douglas were published in the Illinois *State Register* on the 16th of October, 1854, as being the resolutions of an anti-Nebraska Convention which had sat in that same month of October, at Springfield.   But it is also true that the publication in the *Register* was a forgery then, and the question is still behind, which of the three, if not all of them, committed that forgery. The idea that it was done by mistake is absurd. The article in the Illinois *State Register* contains part of the real proceedings of that Springfield Convention, showing that the writer of the article had the real proceedings before him, and purposely threw out the genuine resolutions passed by the Convention and fraudulently substituted the others.   Lanphier then, as now, was the editor of the *Register*, so that there seems to be but little room for his escape. But then it is to be borne in mind that Lanphier had less interest in the object of that forgery than either of the other two.   The main object of that forgery at that time was to beat Yates and elect Harris to Congress, and that object was known to be exceedingly dear to Judge Douglas at that time.   Harris and Douglas were both in Springfield when the Convention was in session, and although they both left before the fraud appeared in the *Register*, subsequent events show that they have both had their eyes fixed upon that Convention.

The fraud having been apparently successful upon the occasion, both Harris and Douglas have more than once since then been attempting to put it to new uses.   As the fisherman's wife, whose drowned husband was brought home with his body full of eels, said when she was asked what was to be done with him, "*Take the eels out and set him again*," so Harris and Douglas have shown a disposition to take the eels out of that stale fraud by which they gained Harris's election, and set the fraud again more than once. On the 9th of July, 1856, Douglas attempted a repetition of it upon Trumbull on the floor of the Senate of the United States, as will appear from the appendix of the *Congressional Globe* of that date.

On the 9th of August, Harris attempted it again upon Norton in the House of Representatives, as will appear by the same documents,— the appendix to the *Congressional Globe* of that date. On the 21st of August last, all three—Lanphier, Douglas, and Harris—reattempted it upon me at Ottawa. It has been clung to and played out again and again as an exceedingly high trump by this blessed trio. And now that it has been discovered publicly to be a fraud we find that Judge Douglas manifests no surprise at it at all. He makes no complaint of Lanphier, who must have known it to be a fraud from the beginning. He, Lanphier, and Harris are just as cosey now and just as active in the concoction of new schemes as they were before the general discovery of this fraud. Now, all this is very natural if they are all alike guilty in that fraud, and it is very unnatural if any one of them is innocent. Lanphier perhaps insists that the rule of honor among thieves does not quite require him to take all upon himself, and consequently my friend Judge Douglas finds it difficult to make a satisfactory report upon his investigation.

But meanwhile the three are agreed that each is "*a most honorable man.*"

Judge Douglas requires an indorsement of his truth and honor by a re-election to the United States Senate, and he makes and reports against me and against Judge Trumbull, day after day, charges which we know to be utterly untrue, without for a moment seeming to think that this one unexplained fraud, which he promised to investigate, will be the least drawback to his claim to belief. Harris ditto. He asks a re-election to the lower House of Congress without seeming to remember at all that he is involved in this dishonorable fraud! The Illinois *State Register*, edited by Lanphier, then, as now, the central organ of both Harris and Douglas, continues to din the public ear with this assertion, without seeming to suspect that these assertions are at all lacking in title to belief.

After all, the question still recurs upon us, How did that fraud originally get into the *State Register?* Lanphier then, as now, was the editor of that paper. Lanphier knows. Lanphier cannot be ignorant of how and by whom it was originally concocted. Can he be induced to tell, or, if he has told, can Judge Douglas be induced to tell how it originally was concocted? It may be true that Lanphier insists that the two men for whose benefit it was originally devised shall at least bear their share of it! How that is, I do not know, and while it remains unexplained I hope to be pardoned if I insist that the mere fact of Judge Douglas making charges against Trumbull and myself is not quite sufficient evidence to establish them!

While we were at Freeport, in one of these joint discussions, I answered certain interrogatories which Judge Douglas had propounded to me, and then in turn propounded some to him, which he in a sort of way answered. The third one of these interrogatories I have with me, and wish now to make some comments upon it. It was in these words: "If the Supreme Court of the United States shall decide that the States cannot exclude slavery from their limits, are you in favor of acquiescing in, adhering to, and following such decision as a rule of political action?"

To this interrogatory Judge Douglas made no answer in any just sense of the word. He contented himself with sneering at the thought that it was possible for the Supreme Court ever to make such a decision. He sneered at me for propounding the interrogatory. I had not propounded it without some reflection, and I wish now to address to this audience some remarks upon it.

In the second clause of the sixth article, I believe it is, of the Constitution of the United States, we find the following language:

"This Constitution and the laws of the United States which shall be made in pursuance thereof, and all treaties made, or which shall be made, under the authority of the United States, shall be the supreme law of the land; and the judges in every State shall be bound thereby, anything in the Constitution or laws of any State to the contrary notwithstanding."

The essence of the Dred Scott case is compressed into the sentence which I will now read: "Now, as we have already said in an earlier part of this opinion, upon a different point, the right of property in a slave is distinctly and expressly affirmed in the Constitution." I repeat it, "*The right of property in a slave is distinctly and expressly affirmed in the Constitution*"! What is it to be "*affirmed*" in the Constitution? Made firm in the Constitution,—so made that it cannot be separated from the Constitution without breaking the Constitution; durable as the Constitution, and part of the Constitution. Now, remembering the provision of the Constitution which I have read—affirming that that instrument is the supreme law of the land; that the judges of every State shall be bound by it, any law or constitution of any State to the contrary notwithstanding; that the right of property in a slave is affirmed in that Constitution, is made, formed into, and cannot be separated from it without breaking it; durable as the instrument; part of the instrument;—what follows as a short and even syllogistic argument from it? I think it follows, and I submit to the consideration of men capable of arguing whether, as I state it, in syllogistic form, the argument has any fault in it:

Nothing in the Constitution or laws of any State can destroy a right distinctly and expressly affirmed in the Constitution of the United States.

The right of property in a slave is distinctly and expressly affirmed in the Constitution of the United States.

Therefore, nothing in the Constitution or laws of any State can destroy the right of property in a slave.

I believe that no fault can be pointed out in that argument; assuming the truth of the premises, the conclusion, so far as I have capacity at all to understand it, follows inevitably. There is a fault in it as I think, but the fault is not in the reasoning; but the falsehood in fact is a fault of the premises. I believe that the right of property in a slave *is not* distinctly and expressly affirmed in the Constitution, and Judge Douglas thinks it *is*. I believe that the Supreme Court and the advocates of that decision may search in vain for the place in the Constitution where the right of property in a slave is distinctly and expressly affirmed. I say, therefore, that I think one of the premises is not true in fact. But it is true with Judge Douglas. It is true with the Supreme Court who pronounced it. They are estopped from denying it, and being estopped from denying it, the conclusion follows that, the Constitution of the United States being the supreme law, no constitution or law can interfere with it. It being affirmed in the decision that the right of property in a slave is distinctly and expressly affirmed in the Constitution, the conclusion inevitably follows that no State law or constitution can destroy that right. I then say to Judge Douglas and to all others that I think it will take a better answer than a sneer to show that those who have said that the right of property in a slave is distinctly and expressly affirmed in the Constitution, are not prepared to show that no constitution or law can destroy that right. I say I believe it will take a far better argument than a mere sneer to show to the minds of intelligent men that whoever has so said is not prepared, whenever public sentiment is so far advanced as to justify it, to say the other. This is but an opinion, and the opinion of one very humble man; but it is my opinion that the Dred Scott decision, as it is, never would have been made in its present form if the party that made it had not been sustained previously by the elections. My own opinion is, that the new Dred Scott decision, deciding against the right of the people of the States to exclude slavery, will never be made if that party is not sustained by the elections. I believe, further, that it is just as sure to be made as to-morrow is to come, if that party shall be sustained. I have said, upon a former occasion, and I repeat it now, that the course of argument that Judge Douglas makes use of upon this subject (I charge not his motives in this), is preparing the public mind for that new Dred Scott decision. I have asked him again to point out to me the reasons for his first adherence to the Dred Scott decision as it is. I have turned his attention to the fact that General Jackson differed with him in regard to the political obligation of a Supreme Court decision. I have asked his attention to the fact that Jefferson differed with him in regard to the political obligation of a Supreme Court decision. Jefferson said that "Judges are as honest as other men, and not more so." And he said, substantially, that whenever a free people should give up in absolute submission to any department of government, retaining for themselves no appeal from it, their liberties were gone. I have asked his attention to the fact that the Cincinnati platform, upon which he

says he stands, disregards a time-honored decision of
the Supreme Court, in denying the power of Congress to establish a National Bank. I have asked
his attention to the fact that he himself was one of the
most active instruments at one time in breaking
down the Supreme Court of the State of Illinois
because it had made a decision distasteful to him,—a
struggle ending in the remarkable circumstance of his
sitting down as one of the new Judges who were to
overslaugh that decision; getting his title of Judge
in that very way.

So far in this controversy I can get no answer at all
from Judge Douglas upon these subjects. Not one
can I get from him, except that he swells himself up
and says, "All of us who stand by the decision of the
Supreme Court are the friends of the Constitution;
all you fellows that dare question it in any way are
the enemies of the Constitution." Now, in this very
devoted adherence to this decision, in opposition to
all the great political leaders whom he has recognized as leaders, in opposition to his former self and
history, there is something very marked. And the
manner in which he adheres to it,—not as being
right upon the merits, as he conceives (because he
did not discuss that at all), but as being absolutely
obligatory upon every one simply because of the
source from whence it comes, as that which no man
can gainsay, whatever it may be,—this is another
marked feature of his adherence to that decision.
It marks it in this respect, that it commits him to
the next decision, whenever it comes, as being as
obligatory as this one, since he does not investigate

it, and won't inquire whether this opinion is right or wrong.   So he takes the next one without inquiring whether *it* is right or wrong.   He teaches men this doctrine, and in so doing prepares the public mind to take the next decision when it comes, without any inquiry.   In this I think I argue fairly (without questioning motives at all) that Judge Douglas is most ingeniously and powerfully preparing the public mind to take that decision when it comes; and not only so, but he is doing it in various other ways.   In these general maxims about liberty, in his assertions that he "don't care whether slavery is voted up or voted down"; that "whoever wants slavery has a right to have it"; that "upon principles of equality it should be allowed to go everywhere"; that "there is no inconsistency between free and slave institutions"—in this he is also preparing (whether purposely or not) the way for making the institution of slavery national!   I repeat again, for I wish no misunderstanding, that I do not charge that he means it so; but I call upon your minds to inquire, if you were going to get the best instrument you could, and then set it to work in the most ingenious way, to prepare the public mind for this movement, operating in the free States, where there is now an abhorrence · of the institution of slavery, could you find an instrument so capable of doing it as Judge Douglas, or one employed in so apt a way to do it?

I have said once before, and I will repeat it now, that Mr. Clay, when he was once answering an objection to the Colonization Society, that it had a tendency to the ultimate emancipation of the slaves, said that "those who would repress all tendencies to liberty and ultimate emancipation must do more than put down the benevolent efforts of the Colonization Society: they must go back to the era of our liberty and independence, and muzzle the cannon that thunders its annual joyous return; they must blow out the moral lights around us; they must penetrate the human soul, and eradicate the light of reason and the love of liberty!"

And I do think—I repeat, though I said it on a former occasion—that Judge Douglas and whoever, like him, teaches that the negro has no share, humble though it may be, in the Declaration of Independence, is going back to the era of our liberty and independence, and, so far as in him lies, muzzling the cannon that thunders its annual joyous return; that he is blowing out the moral lights around us, when he contends that whoever wants slaves has a right to hold them; that he is penetrating, so far as lies in his power, the human soul, and eradicating the light of reason and the love of liberty, when he is in every possible way preparing the public mind, by his vast influence, for making the institution of slavery perpetual and national.

There is, my friends, only one other point to which I will call your attention for the remaining time that I have left me, and perhaps I shall not occupy the entire time that I have, as that one point may not take me clear through it.

Among the interrogatories that Judge Douglas propounded to me at Freeport, there was one in about this language: "Are you opposed to the acquisition of any further territory to the United

States, unless slavery shall first be prohibited
therein?" I answered, as I thought, in this way:
that I am not generally opposed to the acquisition of
additional territory, and that I would support a
proposition for the acquisition of additional territory according as my supporting it was or was not
calculated to aggravate this slavery question amongst
us. I then proposed to Judge Douglas another interrogatory, which was correlative to that: "Are
you in favor of acquiring additional territory, in
disregard of how it may affect us upon the slavery
question?" Judge Douglas answered,—that is, in
his own way he answered it. I believe that, although
he took a good many words to answer it, it was a
little more fully answered than any other. The substance of his answer was that this country would
continue to expand; that it would need additional
territory; that it was as absurd to suppose that we
could continue upon our present territory, enlarging
in population as we are, as it would be to hoop a
boy twelve years of age, and expect him to grow to
man's size without bursting the hoops. I believe it
was something like that. Consequently, he was in
favor of the acquisition of further territory as fast as
we might need it, in disregard of how it might affect
the slavery question. I do not say this as giving his
exact language, but he said so substantially; and he
would leave the question of slavery, where the territory was acquired, to be settled by the people of the
acquired territory. ["That's the doctrine."] May
be it is; let us consider that for a while. This will
probably, in the run of things, become one of the

concrete manifestations of this slavery question. If
Judge Douglas's policy upon this question succeeds,
and gets fairly settled down, until all opposition is
crushed out, the next thing will be a grab for the
territory of poor Mexico, an invasion of the rich
lands of South America, then the adjoining islands
will follow, each one of which promises additional
slave-fields. And this question is to be left to the
people of those countries for settlement. When we
get Mexico, I don't know whether the Judge will be
in favor of the Mexican people that we get with it
settling that question for themselves and all others;
because we know the Judge has a great horror for
mongrels, and I understand that the people of
Mexico are most decidedly a race of mongrels. I
understand that there is not more than one person
there out of eight who is pure white, and I suppose
from the Judge's previous declaration that when we
get Mexico, or any considerable portion of it, that he
will be in favor of these mongrels settling the question, which would bring him somewhat into collision
with his horror of an inferior race.

It is to be remembered, though, that this power of
acquiring additional territory is a power confided to
the President and the Senate of the United States.
It is a power not under the control of the representatives of the people any further than they, the
President and the Senate, can be considered the representatives of the people. Let me illustrate that by a
case we have in our history. When we acquired the
territory from Mexico in the Mexican War, the House
of Representatives, composed of the immediate

representatives of the people, all the time insisted
that the territory thus to be acquired should be
brought in upon condition that slavery should be
forever prohibited therein, upon the terms and in
the language that slavery had been prohibited from
coming into this country.   That was insisted upon
constantly and never failed to call forth an assurance
that any territory thus acquired should have that
prohibition in it, so far as the House of Representatives was concerned.   But at last the President and
Senate acquired the territory without asking the
House of Representatives anything about it, and
took it without that prohibition.   They have the
power of acquiring territory without the immediate
representatives of the people being called upon to say
anything about it, and thus furnishing a very apt and
powerful means of bringing new territory into the
Union, and, when it is once brought into the country,
involving us anew in this slavery agitation.   It is
therefore, as I think, a very important question for
the consideration of the American people, whether
the policy of bringing in additional territory, without
considering at all how it will operate upon the safety
of the Union in reference to this one great disturbing
element in our national politics, shall be adopted as
the policy of the country.   You will bear in mind that
it is to be acquired, according to the Judge's view, as
fast as it is needed, and the indefinite part of this
proposition is that we have only Judge Douglas and
his class of men to decide how fast it is needed.   We
have no clear and certain way of determining or
demonstrating how fast territory is needed by the

necessities of the country. Whoever wants to go out filibustering, then, thinks that more territory is needed. Whoever wants wider slave-fields feels sure that some additional territory is needed as slave territory. Then it is as easy to show the necessity of additional slave-territory as it is to assert anything that is incapable of absolute demonstration. Whatever motive a man or a set of men may have for making annexation of property or territory, it is very easy to assert, but much less easy to disprove, that it is necessary for the wants of the country.

And now it only remains for me to say that I think it is a very grave question for the people of this Union to consider, whether, in view of the fact that this slavery question has been the only one that has ever endangered our Republican institutions, the only one that has ever threatened or menaced a dissolution of the Union, that has ever disturbed us in such a way as to make us fear for the perpetuity of our liberty,—in view of these facts, I think it is an exceedingly interesting and important question for this people to consider whether we shall engage in the policy of acquiring additional territory, discarding altogether from our consideration, while obtaining new territory, the question how it may affect us in regard to this, the only endangering element to our liberties and national greatness. The Judge's view has been expressed. I, in my answer to his question, have expressed mine. I think it will become an important and practical question. Our views are before the public. I am willing and anxious that they should consider them fully; that they should turn it about and consider the importance of the question, and arrive at a just conclusion as to whether it is or is not wise in the people of this Union, in the acquisition of new territory, to consider whether it will add to the disturbance that is existing amongst us—whether it will add to the one only danger that has ever threatened the perpetuity of the Union or our own liberties. I think it is extremely important that they shall decide, and rightly decide, that question before entering upon that policy.

And now, my friends, having said the little I wish to say upon this head, whether I have occupied the whole of the remnant of my time or not, I believe I could not enter upon any new topic so as to treat it fully, without transcending my time, which I would not for a moment think of doing. I give way to Judge Douglas.

MR. DOUGLAS'S REPLY.

GENTLEMEN: The highest compliment you can pay me during the brief half-hour that I have to conclude is by observing a strict silence. I desire to be heard rather than to be applauded.

The first criticism that Mr. Lincoln makes on my speech was that it was in substance what I have said everywhere else in the State where I have addressed the people. I wish I could say the same of his speech. Why, the reason I complain of him is because he makes one speech north, and another south—because he has one set of sentiments for the Abolition counties, and another set for the counties opposed to Abolitionism. My point of complaint against him is that I cannot induce him to hold up the same standard, to carry the same flag, in all parts of the State. He does not pretend, and no other man will, that I have one set of principles for Galesburgh, and another for Charleston. He does not pretend that I hold to one doctrine in Chicago, and an opposite one in Jonesboro. I have proved that he has a different set of principles for each of these localities. All I asked of him was that he should deliver the speech that he has made here to-day in Coles County instead of in old Knox. It would have settled the question between us in that doubtful county. Here I understand him to reaffirm the doctrine of negro equality, and to assert that by the Declaration of Independence the negro is declared equal to the white man. He tells you to-day that the negro was included in the Declaration of Independence when it asserted that all men were created equal. ["We believe it."] Very well.

Mr. Lincoln asserts to-day, as he did at Chicago, that the negro was included in that clause of the Declaration of Independence which says that all men were created equal and endowed by the Creator with certain inalienable rights, among which are life, liberty, and the pursuit of happiness. If the negro was made his equal and mine, if that equality was established by divine law, and was the negro's inalienable right, how came he to say at Charleston to the Kentuckians residing in that section of our State that the negro was physically inferior to the white man, belonged to an inferior race, and he was for keeping him in that inferior condition. There he gave the people to understand that there was no moral question involved, because, the inferiority being established, it was only a question of degree, and not a question of right; here, to-day, instead of making it a question of degree, he makes it a moral question; says that it is a great crime to hold the negro in that inferior condition. ["He's right."] Is he right now, or was he right in Charleston? ["Both."] He is right, then, sir, in your estimation, not because he is consistent, but because he can trim his principles any way, in any section, so as to secure votes. All I desire of him is that he will declare the same principles in the south that he does in the north.

But did you notice how he answered my position that a man should hold the same doctrines throughout the length and breadth of this Republic? He said, "Would Judge Douglas go to Russia and proclaim the same principles he does here?" I would remind him that Russia is not under the American Constitution. If Russia was a part of the American Republic, under our Federal Constitution, and I was sworn to support the Constitution, I would maintain the same doctrine in Russia that I do in Illinois. The slaveholding States are governed by the same Federal Constitution as ourselves, and hence a man's principles, in order to be in harmony with the Constitution, must be the same in the South as they are in the North, the same in the Free States as they are in the Slave States. Whenever a man advocates one

set of principles in one section, and another set in
another section, his opinions are in violation of the
spirit of the Constitution which he has sworn to support. When Mr. Lincoln went to Congress in 1847
and, laying his hand upon the Holy Evangelists,
made a solemn vow, in the presence of high Heaven,
that he would be faithful to the Constitution, what
did he mean,—the Constitution as he expounds it in
Galesburgh, or the Constitution as he expounds it
in Charleston?

Mr. Lincoln has devoted considerable time to the
circumstance that at Ottawa I read a series of
resolutions as having been adopted at Springfield,
in this State, on the 4th or 5th of October, 1854,
which happened not to have been adopted there.
He has used hard names; has dared to talk about
fraud, about forgery, and has insinuated that there
was a conspiracy between Mr. Lanphier, Mr. Harris,
and myself to perpetrate a forgery. Now, bear in
mind that he does not deny that these resolutions
were adopted in a majority of all the Republican
counties of this State in that year; he does not deny
that they were declared to be the platform of this
Republican party in the first Congressional District,
in the second, in the third, and in many counties of
the fourth, and that they thus became the platform
of his party in a majority of the counties upon which
he now relies for support; he does not deny the
truthfulness of the resolutions, but takes exception
to the *spot* on which they were adopted. He takes to
himself great merit because he thinks they were not
adopted on the right spot for me to use them against

him, just as he was very severe in Congress upon the
Government of his country when he thought that he
had discovered that the Mexican War was not begun
in the right *spot*, and was therefore unjust.   He tries
very hard to make out that there is something very
extraordinary in the place where the thing was done,
and not in the thing itself.   I never believed before
that Abraham Lincoln would be guilty of what he
has done this day in regard to those resolutions.   In
the first place, the moment it was intimated to me
that they had been adopted at Aurora and Rockford
instead of Springfield, I did not wait for him to call
my attention to the fact, but led off, and explained
in my first meeting after the Ottawa debate what the
mistake was, and how it had been made.   I supposed that for an honest man, conscious of his own
rectitude, that explanation would be sufficient.   I
did not wait for him, after the mistake was made, to
call my attention to it, but frankly explained it at
once as an honest man would.   I also gave the
authority on which I had stated that these resolutions were adopted by the Springfield Republican
Convention; that I had seen them quoted by Major
Harris in a debate in Congress, as having been
adopted by the first Republican State Convention in
Illinois, and that I had written to him and asked
him for the authority as to the time and place of
their adoption; that, Major Harris being extremely
ill, Charles H. Lanphier had written to me, for him,
that they were adopted at Springfield on the 5th of
October, 1854, and had sent me a copy of the Springfield paper containing them.   I read them from the

newspaper just as Mr. Lincoln reads the proceedings of meetings held years ago from the newspapers. After giving that explanation, I did not think there was an honest man in the State of Illinois who doubted that I had been·led into the error, if it was such, innocently, in the way I detailed; and I will now say that I do not now believe that there is an honest man on the face of the globe who will not regard with abhorrence and disgust Mr. Lincoln's insinuations of my complicity in that forgery, if it was a forgery. Does Mr. Lincoln wish to push these things to the point of personal difficulties here? I commenced this contest by treating him courteously and kindly; I always spoke of him in words of respect; and in return he has sought and is now seeking to divert public attention from the enormity of his revolutionary principles by impeaching men's sincerity and integrity, and inviting personal quarrels.

I desired to conduct this contest with him like a gentleman; but I spurn the insinuation of complicity and fraud made upon the simple circumstance of an editor of a newspaper having made a mistake as to the place where a thing was done, but not as to the thing itself. These resolutions were the platform of this Republican party of Mr. Lincoln's of that year. They were adopted in a majority of the Republican counties in the State; and when I asked him at Ottawa whether they formed the platform upon which he stood, he did not answer, and I could not get an answer out of him. He then thought, as I thought, that those resolutions were adopted at the

10

Springfield Convention, but excused himself by saying that he was not there when they were adopted,
but had gone to Tazewell court in order to avoid
being present at the Convention.   He saw them published as having been adopted at Springfield, and so
did I, and he knew that if there was a mistake in
regard to them, that I had nothing under heaven to
do with it.   Besides, you find that in all these
northern counties where the Republican candidates
are running pledged to him, that the conventions
which nominated them adopted that identical platform.   One cardinal point in that platform which
he shrinks from is this: that there shall be no more
slave States admitted into the Union, even if the
people want them.   Lovejoy stands pledged against
the admission of any more slave States. ["Right,
so do we."] So do you, you say. Farnsworth
stands pledged against the admission of any more
slave States.   Washburne stands pledged the same
way. The candidate for the Legislature who is
running on Lincoln's ticket in Henderson and
Warren stands committed by his vote in the Legislature to the same thing; and I am informed, but do
not know of the fact, that your candidate here is
also so pledged. ["Hurrah for him! Good!"] Now,
you Republicans all hurrah for him, and for the
doctrine of "no more slave States," and yet Lincoln
tells you that his conscience will not permit him to
sanction that doctrine, and complains because the
resolutions I read at Ottawa made him, as a member
of the party, responsible for sanctioning the doctrine
of no more slave States. You are one way, you

confess, and he is, or pretends to be, the other; and yet you are both governed by *principle* in supporting one another. If it be true, as I have shown it is, that the whole Republican party in the northern part of the State stands committed to the doctrine of no more slave States, and that this same doctrine is repudiated by the Republicans in the other part of the State, I wonder whether Mr. Lincoln and his party do not present the case which he cited from the Scriptures, of a house divided against itself which cannot stand! I desire to know what are Mr. Lincoln's principles and the principles of his party. I hold, and the party with which I am identified hold, that the people of each State, old and new, have the right to decide the slavery question for themselves; and when I used the remark that I did not care whether slavery was voted up or down, I used it in the connection that I was for allowing Kansas to do just as she pleased on the slavery question. I said that I did not care whether they voted slavery up or down, because they had the right to do as they pleased on the question, and therefore my action would not be controlled by any such consideration. Why cannot Abraham Lincoln, and the party with which he acts, speak out their principles so that they may be understood? Why do they claim to be one thing in one part of the State, and another in the other part? Whenever I allude to the Abolition doctrines, which he considers a slander to be charged with being in favor of, you all indorse them, and hurrah for them, not knowing that your candidate is ashamed to acknowledge them.

I have a few words to say upon the Dred Scott decision, which has troubled the brain of Mr. Lincoln so much. He insists that that decision would carry slavery into the free States, notwithstanding that the decision says directly the opposite, and goes into a long argument to make you believe that I am in favor of, and would sanction, the doctrine that would allow slaves to be brought here and held as slaves contrary to our Constitution and laws. Mr. Lincoln knew better when he asserted this; he knew that one newspaper, and, so far as is within my knowledge, but one, ever asserted that doctrine, and that I was the first man in either House of Congress that read that article in debate, and denounced it on the floor of the Senate as revolutionary. When the Washington *Union*, on the 17th of last November, published an article to that effect, I branded it at once, and denounced it; and hence the *Union* has been pursuing me ever since. Mr. Toombs, of Georgia, replied to me, and said that there was not a man in any of the slave States south of the Potomac River that held any such doctrine. Mr. Lincoln knows that there is not a member of the Supreme Court who holds that doctrine; he knows that every one of them, as shown by their opinions, holds the reverse. Why this attempt, then, to bring the Supreme Court into disrepute among the people? It looks as if there was an effort being made to destroy public confidence in the highest judicial tribunal on earth. Suppose he succeeds in destroying public confidence in the court, so that the people will not respect its decisions, but will feel at liberty to disregard them and resist

the laws of the land, what will he have gained? He
will have changed the government from one of laws
into that of a mob, in which the strong arm of violence will be substituted for the decisions of the courts
of justice. He complains because I did not go into
an argument reviewing Chief Justice Taney's opinion,
and the other opinions of the different judges, to
determine whether their reasoning is right or wrong
on the questions of law. What use would that be?
He wants to take an appeal from the Supreme Court
to this meeting, to determine whether the questions
of law were decided properly. He is going to appeal
from the Supreme Court of the United States to every
town meeting, in the hope that he can excite a prejudice against that court, and on the wave of that
prejudice ride into the Senate of the United States,
when he could not get there on his own principles or
his own merits. Suppose he should succeed in getting
into the Senate of the United States, what then will
he have to do with the decision of the Supreme Court
in the Dred Scott case? Can he reverse that decision when he gets there? Can he act upon it? Has
the Senate any right to reverse it or revise it? He
will not pretend that it has. Then why drag the
matter into this contest, unless for the purpose of
making a false issue, by which he can direct public
attention from the real issue.

He has cited General Jackson in justification of the
war he is making on the decision of the court. Mr.
Lincoln misunderstands the history of the country if
he believes there is any parallel in the two cases. It
is true that the Supreme Court once decided that if

a Bank of the United States was a necessary fiscal agent of the government, it was constitutional, and if not, that it was unconstitutional, and also, that whether or not it was necessary for that purpose was a political question for Congress, and not a judicial one for the courts to determine. Hence the court would not determine the bank unconstitutional. Jackson respected the decision, obeyed the law, executed it, and carried it into effect during its existence; but after the charter of the bank expired, and a proposition was made to create a new bank, General Jackson said, "It is unnecessary and improper, and therefore I am against it on constitutional grounds as well as those of expediency." Is Congress bound to pass every act that is constitutional? Why, there are a thousand things that are constitutional, but yet are inexpedient and unnecessary, and you surely would not vote for them merely because you had the right to? And because General Jackson would not do a thing which he had a right to do, but did not deem expedient or proper, Mr. Lincoln is going to justify himself in doing that which he has no right to do. I ask him whether he is not bound to respect and obey the decisions of the Supreme Court as well as I? The Constitution has created that court to decide all constitutional questions in the last resort; and when such decisions have been made, they become the law of the land, and you, and he, and myself, and every other good citizen, are bound by them. Yet he argues that I am bound by their decisions, and he is not. He says that their decisions are binding on Democrats, but not on Republicans. Are not Republicans bound by the laws of the land as well as Democrats? And when the court has fixed the construction of the Constitution on the validity of a given law, is not their decision binding upon Republicans as well as upon Democrats? Is it possible that you Republicans have the right to raise your mobs and oppose the laws of the land and the constituted authorities, and yet hold us Democrats bound to obey them? My time is within half a minute of expiring, and all I have to say is, that I stand by the laws of the land. I stand by the Constitution as our fathers made it, by the laws as they are enacted, and by the decisions of the court, upon all points within their jurisdiction, as they are pronounced by the highest tribunal on earth; and any man who resists these must resort to mob law and violence to overturn the government of laws.

SIXTH JOINT DEBATE, AT QUINCY,

OCTOBER 13, 1858.

MR. LINCOLN'S SPEECH.

LADIES AND GENTLEMEN: I have had no immediate conference with Judge Douglas, but I will venture to say that he and I will perfectly agree that your entire silence, both when I speak and when he speaks, will be most agreeable to us.

In the month of May, 1856, the elements in the State of Illinois which have since been consolidated into the Republican party assembled together in a State Convention at Bloomington. They adopted at that time what, in political language, is called a platform. In June of the same year the elements of the Republican party in the nation assembled together in a National Convention at Philadelphia. They adopted what is called the National Platform. In June, 1858,—the present year,—the Republicans of Illinois reassembled at Springfield, in State Convention, and adopted again their platform, as I suppose not differing in any essential particular from either of the former ones, but perhaps adding something in relation to the new developments of political progress in the country.

The Convention that assembled in June last did me the honor, if it be one, and I esteem it such, to nominate me as their candidate for the United States

Senate. I have supposed that, in entering upon this canvass, I stood generally upon these platforms. We are now met together on the 13th of October of the same year, only four months from the adoption of the last platform, and I am unaware that in this canvass, from the beginning until to-day, any one of our adversaries has taken hold of our platforms, or laid his finger upon anything that he calls wrong in them.

In the very first one of these joint discussions between Senator Douglas and myself, Senator Douglas, without alluding at all to these platforms, or any one of them, of which I have spoken, attempted to hold me responsible for a set of resolutions passed long before the meeting of either one of these conventions of which I have spoken. And as a ground for holding me responsible for these resolutions, he assumed that they had been passed at a State Convention of the Republican party, and that I took part in that Convention. It was discovered afterward that this was erroneous, that the resolutions which he endeavored to hold me responsible for had not been passed by any State Convention anywhere, had not been passed at Springfield, where he supposed they had, or assumed that they had, and that they had been passed in no convention in which I had taken part. The Judge, nevertheless, was not willing to give up the point that he was endeavoring to make upon me, and he therefore thought to still hold me to the point that he was endeavoring to make, by showing that the resolutions that he read had been passed at a local convention in the northern part of the State, although it was not a local convention that embraced my residence at all, nor one that reached, as I suppose, nearer than one hundred and fifty or two hundred miles of where I was when it met, nor one in which I took any part at all. He also introduced other resolutions, passed at other meetings, and by combining the whole, although they were all antecedent to the two State Conventions. and the one National Convention I have mentioned, still he insisted, and now insists, as I understand, that I am in some way responsible for them.

At Jonesboro, on our third meeting, I insisted to the Judge that I was in no way rightfully held responsible for the proceedings of this local meeting or convention, in which I had taken no part, and in which I was in no way embraced; but I insisted to him that if he thought I was responsible for every man or every set of men everywhere, who happen to be my friends, the rule ought to work both ways, and he ought to be responsible for the acts and resolutions of all men or sets of men who were or are now his supporters and friends, and gave him a pretty long string of resolutions, passed by men who are now his friends, and announcing doctrines for which he does not desire to be held responsible.

This still does not satisfy Judge Douglas. He still adheres to his proposition, that I am responsible for what some of my friends in different parts of the State have done, but that he is not responsible for what his have done. At least, so I understand him. But in addition to that, the Judge, at our meeting in Galesburgh, last week, undertakes to establish that

I am guilty of a species of double dealing with the public; that I make speeches of a certain sort in the north, among the Abolitionists, which I would not make in the south, and that I make speeches of a certain sort in the south which I would not make in the north. I apprehend, in the course I have marked out for myself, that I shall not have to dwell at very great length upon this subject.

As this was done in the Judge's opening speech at Galesburgh, I had an opportunity, as I had the middle speech then, of saying something in answer to it. He brought forward a quotation or two from a speech of mine delivered at Chicago, and then, to contrast with it, he brought forward an extract from a speech of mine at Charleston, in which he insisted that I was greatly inconsistent, and insisted that his conclusion followed, that I was playing a double part, and speaking in one region one way, and in another region another way. I have not time now to dwell on this as long as I would like, and wish only now to requote that portion of my speech at Charleston which the Judge quoted, and then make some comments upon it. This he quotes from me as being delivered at Charleston, and I believe correctly:

"I will say, then, that I am not, nor ever have been, in favor of bringing about in any way the social and political equality of the white and black races; that I am not, nor ever have been, in favor of making voters or jurors of negroes, nor of qualifying them to hold office, nor to intermarry with white people; and I will say, in addition to this, that there is a physical difference between the white and black races which will forever forbid

the two races living together on terms of social and
political equality. And inasmuch as they cannot so
live while they do remain together, there must be the
position of superior and inferior. I am as much as any
other man in favor of having the superior position assigned to the white race."

This, I believe, is the entire quotation from the
Charleston speech, as Judge Douglas made it. His
comments are as follows:

"Yes, here you find men who hurrah for Lincoln, and
say he is right when he discards all distinction between
races, or when he declares that he discards the doctrine
that there is such a thing as a superior and inferior race;
and Abolitionists are required and expected to vote for
Mr. Lincoln because he goes for the equality of races,
holding that in the Declaration of Independence the
white man and negro were declared equal, and endowed
by divine law with equality. And down South, with
the old-line Whigs, with the Kentuckians, the Virginians,
and the Tennesseeans, he tells you that there is a physical difference between the races, making the one superior,
the other inferior, and he is in favor of maintaining the
superiority of the white race over the negro."

Those are the Judges comments. Now, I wish to
show you that a month, or only lacking three days of
a month, before I made the speech at Charleston,
which the Judge quotes from, he had himself heard
me say substantially the same thing. It was in our
first meeting, at Ottawa—and I will say a word about
where it was, and the atmosphere it was in, after
a while—but at our first meeting, at Ottawa, I read

an extract from an old speech of mine, made nearly
four years ago, not merely to show my sentiments, but
to show that my sentiments were long entertained and
openly expressed; in which extract I expressly declared that my own feelings would not admit a social
and political equality between the white and black
races, and that even if my own feelings would admit
of it, I still knew that the public sentiment of the
country would not, and that such a thing was an
utter impossibility, or substantially that. That
extract from my old speech the reporters by some
sort of accident passed over, and it was not reported.
I lay no blame upon anybody. I suppose they
thought that I would hand it over to them, and
dropped reporting while I was reading it, but afterward went away without getting it from me. At
the end of that quotation from my old speech, which
I read at Ottawa, I made the comments which were
reported at that time, and which I will now read, and
ask you to notice how very nearly they are the same
as Judge Douglas says were delivered by me down
in Egypt. After reading, I added these words:

"Now, gentlemen, I don't want to read at any great
length; but this is the true complexion of all I have ever
said in regard to the institution of slavery or the black
race, and this is the whole of it: anything that argues
me into his idea of perfect social and political equality
with the negro, is but a specious and fantastical arrangement of words by which a man can prove a horse-
chestnut to be a chestnut horse. I will say here, while
upon this subject, that I have no purpose, directly or
indirectly, to interfere with the institution in the States

where it exists. I believe I have no right to do so. I have no inclination to do so. I have no purpose to introduce political and social equality between the white and black races. There is a physical difference between the two which, in my judgment, will probably forever forbid their living together on the footing of perfect equality; and inasmuch as it becomes a necessity that there must be a difference, I, as well as Judge Douglas, am in favor of the race to which I belong having the superior position. I have never said anything to the contrary, but I hold that, notwithstanding all this, there is no reason in the world why the negro is not entitled to all the rights enumerated in the Declaration of Independence,—the right of life, liberty, and the pursuit of happiness. I hold that he is as much entitled to these as the white man. I agree with Judge Douglas that he is not my equal in many respects, certainly not in color, perhaps not in intellectual and moral endowments; but in the right to eat the bread, without the leave of anybody else, which his own hand earns, he is my equal and the equal of Judge Douglas, and the equal of every other man."

I have chiefly introduced this for the purpose of meeting the Judge's charge that the quotation he took from my Charleston speech was what I would say down South among the Kentuckians, the Virginians, etc., but would not say in the regions in which was supposed to be more of the Abolition element. I now make this comment: That speech from which I have now read the quotation, and which is there given correctly—perhaps too much so for good taste—was made away up North in the Abolition District of this State *par excellence*, in the

Lovejoy District, in the personal presence of Lovejoy, for he was on the stand with us when I made it. It had been made and put in print in that region only three days less than a month before the speech made at Charleston, the like of which Judge Douglas thinks I would not make where there was any Abolition element. I only refer to this matter to say that I am altogether unconscious of having attempted any double-dealing anywhere; that upon one occasion I may say one thing, and leave other things unsaid, and *vice versa*, but that I have said anything on one occasion that is inconsistent with what I have said elsewhere, I deny,—at least I deny it so far as the intention is concerned. I find that I have devoted to this topic a larger portion of my time than I had intended. I wished to show, but I will pass it upon this occasion, that in the sentiment I have occasionally advanced upon the Declaration of Independence I am entirely borne out by the sentiments advanced by our old Whig leader, Henry Clay, and I have the book here to show it from; but because I have already occupied more time than I intended to do on that topic, I pass over it.

At Galesburgh, I tried to show that by the Dred Scott decision, pushed to its legitimate consequences, slavery would be established in all the States as well as in the Territories. I did this because, upon a former occasion, I had asked Judge Douglas whether, if the Supreme Court should make a decision declaring that the States had not the power to exclude slavery from their limits, he would adopt and follow that decision as a rule of political action; and because he had not directly answered that question, but had merely contented himself with sneering at it, I again introduced it, and tried to show that the conclusion that I stated followed inevitably and logically from the proposition already decided by the court. Judge Douglas had the privilege of replying to me at Galesburgh, and again he gave me no direct answer as to whether he would or would not sustain such a decision if made. I give him his third chance to say yes or no. He is not obliged to do either,— probably he will not do either; but I give him the third chance. I tried to show then that this result, this conclusion, inevitably followed from the point already decided by the court. The Judge, in his reply, again sneers at the thought of the court making any such decision, and in the course of his remarks upon this subject uses the language which I will now read. Speaking of me, the Judge says: "He goes on and insists that the Dred Scott decision would carry slavery into the free States, notwithstanding the decision itself says the contrary." And he adds: "Mr. Lincoln knows that there is no member of the Supreme Court that holds that doctrine. He knows that every one of them in their opinions held the reverse."

I especially introduce this subject again for the purpose of saying that I have the Dred Scott decision here, and I will thank Judge Douglas to lay his finger upon the place in the entire opinions of the court where any one of them "says the contrary." It is very hard to affirm a negative with entire confidence. I say, however, that I have examined that decision with a good deal of care, as a lawyer examines a decision, and, so far as I have been able to do so, the court has nowhere in its opinions said that the States have the power to exclude slavery, nor have they used other language substantially that. I also say, so far as I can find, not one of the concurring judges has said that the States can exclude slavery, nor said anything that was substantially that. The nearest approach that any one of them has made to it, so far as I can find, was by Judge Nelson, and the approach he made to it was exactly, in substance, the Nebraska Bill,—that the States had the exclusive power over the question of slavery, so far as they are not limited by the Constitution of the United States. I asked the question, therefore, if the non-concurring judges, McLean or Curtis, had asked to get an express declaration that the States could absolutely exclude slavery from their limits, what reason have we to believe that it would not have been voted down by the majority of the judges, just as Chase's amendment was voted down by Judge Douglas and his compeers when it was offered to the Nebraska Bill.

Also, at Galesburgh, I said something in regard to those Springfield resolutions that Judge Douglas had attempted to use upon me at Ottawa, and commented at some length upon the fact that they were, as presented, not genuine. Judge Douglas in his reply to me seemed to be somewhat exasperated. He said he would never have believed that Abraham Lincoln, as he kindly called me, would have attempted such a thing as I had attempted upon that

11

occasion; and among other expressions which he used toward me, was that I dared to say forgery,—that I had *dared* to say forgery [turning to Judge Douglas]. Yes, Judge, I did dare to say forgery. But in this political canvass the Judge ought to remember that I was not the first who *dared* to say forgery. At Jacksonville, Judge Douglas made a speech in answer to something said by Judge Trumbull, and at the close of what he said upon that subject, he *dared* to say that Trumbull had forged his evidence. He said, too, that he should not concern himself with Trumbull any more, but thereafter he should hold Lincoln responsible for the slanders upon him. When I met him at Charleston after that, although I think that I should not have noticed the subject if he had not said he would hold me responsible for it, I spread out before him the statements of the evidence that Judge Trumbull had used, and I asked Judge Douglas, piece by piece, to put his finger upon one piece of all that evidence that he would say was a forgery! When I went through with each and every piece, Judge Douglas did not *dare* then to say that any piece of it was a forgery. So it seems that there are some things that Judge Douglas dares to do, and some that he dares not to do.

A voice: It's the same thing with you.

Mr. LINCOLN: Yes, sir, it's the same thing with me. I do dare to say forgery when it's true, and don't dare to say forgery when it's false. Now I will say here to this audience and to Judge Douglas I have not dared to say he committed a forgery, and I never shall until I know it; but I did dare to say—

just to suggest to the Judge—that a forgery had been committed, which by his own showing had been traced to him and two of his friends. I dared to suggest to him that he had expressly promised in one of his public speeches to investigate that matter, and I dared to suggest to him that there was an implied promise that when he investigated it he would make known the result. I dared to suggest to the Judge that he could not expect to be quite clear of suspicion of that fraud, for since the time that promise was made he had been with those friends, and had not kept his promise in regard to the investigation and the report upon it. I am not a very daring man, but I dared that much, Judge, and I am not much scared about it yet. When the Judge says he would n't have believed of Abraham Lincoln that he would have made such an attempt as that he reminds me of the fact that he entered upon this canvass with the purpose to treat me courteously; that touched me somewhat. It sets me to thinking. I was aware, when it was first agreed that Judge Douglas and I were to have these seven joint discussions, that they were the successive acts of a drama, perhaps I should say, to be enacted, not merely in the face of audiences like this, but in the face of the nation, and to some extent, by my relation to him, and not from anything in myself, in the face of the world; and I am anxious that they should be conducted with dignity and in the good temper which would be befitting the vast audiences before which it was conducted. But when Judge Douglas got home from Washington and made his first speech in Chicago,

the evening afterward I made some sort of a reply to
it. His second speech was made at Bloomington, in
which he commented upon my speech at Chicago
and said that I had used language ingeniously con-
trived to conceal my intentions,—or words to that
effect. Now, I understand that this is an imputation
upon my veracity and my candor. I do not know
what the Judge understood by it, but in our first discussion, at Ottawa, he led off by charging a bargain,
somewhat corrupt in its character, upon Trumbull
and myself,—that we had entered into a bargain,
one of the terms of which was that Trumbull was
to Abolitionize the old Democratic party, and I
(Lincoln) was to Abolitionize the old Whig party; I
pretending to be as good an old-line Whig as ever.
Judge Douglas may not understand that he implicated my truthfulness and my honor when he said
I was doing one thing and pretending another; and
I misunderstood him if he thought he was treating
me in a dignified way, as a man of honor and truth,
as he now claims he was disposed to treat me.
Even after that time, at Galesburgh, when he brings
forward an extract from a speech made at Chicago,
and an extract from a speech made at Charleston,
to prove that I was trying to play a double part,—
that I was trying to cheat the public, and get votes
upon one set of principles at one place, and upon
another set of principles at another place,—I do not
understand but what he impeaches my honor, my
veracity, and my candor; and because *he* does this, I
do not understand that I am bound, if I see a truth-
ful ground for it, to keep my hands off of him. As

soon as I learned that Judge Douglas was disposed to
treat me in this way, I signified in one of my speeches
that I should be driven to draw upon whatever of
humble resources I might have,—to adopt a new
course with him. I was not entirely sure that I
should be able to hold my own with him, but I at
least had the purpose made to do as well as I could
upon him; and now I say that I will not be the first
to cry "Hold." I think it originated with the Judge,
and when he quits, I probably will. But I shall not
ask any favors at all. He asks me, or he asks the
audience, if I wish to push this matter to the point of
personal difficulty. I tell him, no. He did not make
a mistake, in one of his early speeches, when he
called me an "amiable" man, though perhaps he did
when he called me an "intelligent" man. It really
hurts me very much to suppose that I have wronged
anybody on earth. I again tell him, no! I very
much prefer, when this canvass shall be over, however it may result, that we at least part without any
bitter recollections of personal difficulties.

The Judge, in his concluding speech at Galesburgh,
says that I was pushing this matter to a personal
difficulty, to avoid the responsibility for the enormity
of my principles. I say to the Judge and this audience, now, that I will again state our principles, as
well as I hastily can, in all their enormity, and if the
Judge hereafter chooses to confine himself to a war
upon these principles, he will probably not find me
departing from the same course.

We have in this nation this element of domestic
slavery. It is a matter of absolute certainty that it

is a disturbing element. It is the opinion of all the great men who have expressed an opinion upon it, that it is a dangerous element. We keep up a controversy in regard to it. That controversy necessarily springs from difference of opinion; and if we can learn exactly—can reduce to the lowest elements —what that difference of opinion is, we perhaps shall be better prepared for discussing the different systems of policy that we would propose in regard to that disturbing element. I suggest that the difference of opinion, reduced to its lowest of terms, is no other than the difference between the men who think slavery a wrong and those who do not think it wrong. The Republican party think it wrong; we think it is a moral, a social, and a political wrong. We think it as a wrong not confining itself merely to the persons or the States where it exists, but that it is a wrong in its tendency, to say the least, that extends itself to the existence of the whole nation. Because we think it wrong, we propose a course of policy that shall deal with it as a wrong. We deal with it as with any other wrong, in so far as we can prevent its growing any larger, and so deal with it that in the run of time there may be some promise of an end to it. We have a due regard to the actual presence of it amongst us, and the difficulties of getting rid of it in any satisfactory way, and all the constitutional obligations thrown about it. I suppose that in reference both to its actual existence in the nation, and to our constitutional obligations, we have no right at all to disturb it in the States where it exists, and we profess that we have no more inclination to disturb it than we have the right to do it. We go further than that: we don't propose to disturb it where, in one instance, we think the Constitution would permit us. We think the Constitution would permit us to disturb it in the District of Columbia. Still, we do not propose to do that, unless it should be in terms which I don't suppose the nation is very likely soon to agree to,—the terms of making the emancipation gradual, and compensating the unwilling owners. Where we suppose we have the constitutional right, we restrain ourselves in reference to the actual existence of the institution and the difficulties thrown about it. We also oppose it as an evil so far as it seeks to spread itself. We insist on the policy that shall restrict it to its present limits. We don't suppose that in doing this we violate anything due to the actual presence of the institution, or anything due to the constitutional guaranties thrown around it.

We oppose the Dred Scott decision in a certain way, upon which I ought perhaps to address you a few words. We do not propose that when Dred Scott has been decided to be a slave by the court, we, as a mob, will decide him to be free. We do not propose that, when any other one, or one thousand, shall be decided by that court to be slaves, we will in any violent way disturb the rights of property thus settled; but we nevertheless do oppose that decision as a political rule which shall be binding on the voter to vote for nobody who thinks it wrong, which shall be binding on the members of Congress or the President to favor no measure that does not actually concur with the principles of that decision. We do not propose to be bound by it as a political rule in that way, because we think it lays the foundation, not merely of enlarging and spreading out what we consider an evil, but it lays the foundation for spreading that evil into the States themselves. We propose so resisting it as to have it reversed if we can, and a new judicial rule established upon this subject.

I will add this: that if there be any man who does not believe that slavery is wrong in the three aspects which I have mentioned, or in any one of them, that man is misplaced, and ought to leave us; while on the other hand, if there be any man in the Republican party who is impatient over the necessity springing from its actual presence, and is impatient of the constitutional guaranties thrown around it, and would act in disregard of these, he too is misplaced, standing with us. He will find his place somewhere else; for we have a due regard, so far as we are capable of understanding them, for all these things. This, gentlemen, as well as I can give it, is a plain statement of our principles in all their enormity.

I will say now that there is a sentiment in the country contrary to me,—a sentiment which holds that slavery is not wrong, and therefore it goes for the policy that does not propose dealing with it as a wrong. That policy is the Democratic policy, and that sentiment is the Democratic sentiment. If there be a doubt in the mind of any one of this vast audience that this is really the central idea of the Democratic party in relation to this subject, I ask

him to bear with me while I state a few things tending, as I think, to prove that proposition. In the
first place, the leading man—I think I may do my
friend Judge Douglas the honor of calling him such—
advocating the present Democratic policy never himself says it is wrong. He has the high distinction,
so far as I know, of never having said slavery is either
right or wrong. Almost everybody else says one or
the other, but the Judge never does. If there be a
man in the Democratic party who thinks it is wrong,
and yet clings to that party, I suggest to him, in the
first place, that his leader don't talk as he does, for
he never says that it is wrong. In the second place,
I suggest to him that if he will examine the policy
proposed to be carried forward, he will find that he
carefully excludes the idea that there is anything
wrong in it. If you will examine the arguments
that are made on it, you will find that every one
carefully excludes the idea that there is anything
wrong in slavery. Perhaps that Democrat who
says he is as much opposed to slavery as I am will
tell me that I am wrong about this. I wish him to
examine his own course in regard to this matter a
moment, and then see if his opinion will not be
changed a little. You say it is wrong; but don't
you constantly object to anybody else saying so?
Do you not constantly argue that this is not the
right place to oppose it? You say it must not be
opposed in the free States, because slavery is not
here; it must not be opposed in the slave States,
because it is there; it must not be opposed in
politics, because that will make a fuss; it must not

be opposed in the pulpit, because it is not religion. Then where is the place to oppose it? There is no suitable place to oppose it. There is no place in the country to oppose this evil overspreading the continent, which you say yourself is coming. Frank Blair and Gratz Brown tried to get up a system of gradual emancipation in Missouri, had an election in August, and got beat, and you, Mr. Democrat, threw up your hat, and hallooed "Hurrah for Democracy!" So I say, again, that in regard to the arguments that are made, when Judge Douglas says he "don't care whether slavery is voted up or voted down," whether he means that as an individual expression of sentiment, or only as a sort of statement of his views on national policy, it is alike true to say that he can thus argue logically if he don't see anything wrong in it; but he cannot say so logically if he admits that slavery is wrong. He cannot say that he would as soon see a wrong voted up as voted down. When Judge Douglas says that whoever or whatever community wants slaves, they have a right to have them, he is perfectly logical, if there is nothing wrong in the institution; but if you admit that it is wrong, he cannot logically say that anybody has a right to do wrong. When he says that slave property and horse and hog property are alike to be allowed to go into the Territories, upon the principles of equality, he is reasoning truly, if there is no difference between them as property; but if the one is property held rightfully, and the other is wrong, then there is no equality between the right and wrong; so that, turn it in any way you can, in all the arguments sustaining the Democratic policy, and in that policy itself, there is a careful, studied exclusion of the idea that there is anything wrong in slavery. Let us understand this. I am not, just here, trying to prove that we are right, and they are wrong. I have been stating where we and they stand, and trying to show what is the real difference between us; and I now say that whenever we can get the question distinctly stated, can get all these men who believe that slavery is in some of these respects wrong to stand and act with us in treating it as a wrong,—then, and not till then, I think we will in some way come to an end of this slavery agitation.

MR. DOUGLAS'S REPLY.

LADIES AND GENTLEMEN: Permit me to say that unless silence is observed it will be impossible for me to be heard by this immense crowd, and my friends can confer no higher favor upon me than by omitting all expressions of applause or approbation. I desire to be heard rather than to be applauded. I wish to address myself to your reason, your judgment, your sense of justice, and not to your passions.

I regret that Mr. Lincoln should have deemed it proper for him again to indulge in gross personalities and base insinuations in regard to the Springfield resolutions. It has imposed upon me the necessity of using some portion of my time for the purpose of calling your attention to the facts of the case, and it will then be for you to say what you think of a man who can predicate such a charge upon the circumstances as he has in this. I had seen the platform adopted by a Republican Congressional Convention held in Aurora, the Second Congressional District, in September, 1854, published as purporting to be the platform of the Republican party. That platform declared that the Republican party was pledged never to admit another slave State into the Union, and also that it was pledged to prohibit slavery in all the Territories of the United States, not only all that we then had, but all that we should thereafter acquire, and to repeal unconditionally the Fugitive Slave law, abolish slavery in the District of Columbia, and prohibit the slave-trade between the different States. These and other articles against slavery were contained in this platform, and unanimously adopted by the Republican Congressional Convention in that district. I had also seen that the Republican Congressional Conventions at Rockford, in the First District, and at Bloomington, in the Third, had adopted the same platform that year, nearly word for word, and had declared it to be the platform of the Republican party. I had noticed that Major Thomas L. Harris, a member of Congress from the Springfield District, had referred to that platform in a speech in Congress as having been adopted by the first Republican State Convention which assembled in Illinois. When I had occasion to use the fact in this canvass, I wrote to Major Harris to know on what day that Convention was held, and to ask him to send me its proceedings. He being sick, Charles H. Lanphier answered my

letter by sending me the published proceedings of
the Convention held at Springfield on the 5th of
October, 1854, as they appeared in the report of the
State Register. I read those resolutions from that
newspaper the same as any of you would refer back
and quote any fact from the files of a newspaper
which had published it. Mr. Lincoln pretends that
after I had so quoted those resolutions he discovered that they had never been adopted at Springfield. He does not deny their adoption by the Republican party at Aurora, at Bloomington, and at
Rockford, and by nearly all the Republican County
Conventions in northern Illinois where his party is
in a majority, but merely because they were not
adopted on the "*spot*" on which I said they were, he
chooses to quibble about the place rather than meet
and discuss the merits of the resolutions themselves.
I stated when I quoted them that I did so from the
State Register. I gave my authority. Lincoln believed at the time, as he has since admitted, that
they had been adopted at Springfield, as published.
Does he believe now that I did not tell the truth
when I quoted those resolutions? He knows, in his
heart, that I quoted them in good faith, believing
at the time that they had been adopted at Springfield. I would consider myself an infamous wretch,
if, under such circumstances, I could charge any man
with being a party to a trick or a fraud. And I will
tell him, too, that it will not do to charge a forgery
on Charles H. Lanphier or Thomas L. Harris. No
man an earth, who knows them, and knows Lincoln,
would take his oath against their word. There are

not two men in the State of Illinois who have higher
characters for truth, for integrity, for moral character
and for elevation of tone, as gentlemen, than Mr.
Lanphier and Mr. Harris.   Any man who attempts
to make such charges as Mr. Lincoln has indulged in
against them, only proclaims himself a slanderer.

I will now show you that I stated with entire
fairness, as soon as it was made known to me, that
there was a mistake about the spot where the resolutions had been adopted, although their truthfulness,
as a declaration of the principles of the Republican
party, had not and could not be questioned.   I did
not wait for Lincoln to point out the mistake, but
the moment I discovered it, I made a speech, and
published it to the world, correcting the error.   I
corrected it myself, as a gentleman and an honest
man, and as I always feel proud to do when I have
made a mistake.   I wish Mr. Lincoln could show
that he has acted with equal fairness and truthfulness
when I have convinced him that he has been mistaken.   I will give you an illustration to show you
how he acts in a similar case: In a speech at Springfield, he charged Chief Justice Taney and his associates, President Pierce, President Buchanan, and
myself, with having entered into a conspiracy at the
time the Nebraska Bill was introduced, by which the
Dred Scott decision was to be made by the Supreme
Court, in order to carry slavery everywhere under
the Constitution.   I called his attention to the fact
that at the time alluded to, to wit, the introduction
of the Nebraska Bill, it was not possible that such a
conspiracy could have been entered into, for the

reason that the Dred Scott case had never been
taken before the Supreme Court, and was not taken
before it for a year after; and I asked him to take
back that charge. Did he do it? I showed him
that it was impossible that the charge could be true;
I proved it by the record; and I then called upon
him to retract his false charge. What was his
answer? Instead of coming out like an honest man
and doing so, he reiterated the charge, and said that
if the case had not gone up to the Supreme Court from
the courts of Missouri at the time he charged that
the judges of the Supreme Court entered into the
conspiracy, yet, that there was an understanding
with the Democratic owners of Dred Scott that they
would take it up. I have since asked him who the
Democratic owners of Dred Scott were, but he could
not tell, and why? Because there were no such
Democratic owners in existence. Dred Scott at the
time was owned by the Rev. Dr. Chaffee, an Abolition member of Congress, of Springfield, Massachusetts, in right of his wife. He was owned by one of
Lincoln's friends, and not by Democrats at all; his
case was conducted in court by Abolition lawyers, so
that both the prosecution and the defence were in
the hands of the Abolition political friends of Mr.
Lincoln. Notwithstanding I thus proved by the
record that his charge against the Supreme Court
was false, instead of taking it back, he resorted to
another false charge to sustain the infamy of it. He
also charged President Buchanan with having been
a party to the conspiracy. I directed his attention
to the fact that the charge could not possibly be

true, for the reason that at the time specified, Mr.
Buchanan was not in America, but was three thousand miles off, representing the United States at the
Court of St. James, and had been there for a year
previous, and did not return until three years afterward. Yet I never could get Mr. Lincoln to take
back his false charge, although I have called upon
him over and over again. He refuses to do it, and
either remains silent or resorts to other tricks to try
and palm his slander off on the country. Therein
you will find the difference between Mr. Lincoln and
myself. When I make a mistake, as an honest man
I correct it without being asked to do so; but when
he makes a false charge, he sticks to it, and never
corrects it. One word more in regard to these
resolutions: I quoted them at Ottawa merely to ask
Mr. Lincoln whether he stood on that platform.
That was the purpose for which I quoted them. I
did not think that I had a right to put idle questions
to him, and I first laid a foundation for my questions
by showing that the principles which I wished him
either to affirm or deny had been adopted by some
portion of his friends, at least, as their creed. Hence
I read the resolutions and put the questions to
him, and he then refused to answer them. Subsequently, one week afterward, he did answer a part of
them, but the others he has not answered up to this
day.

Now, let me call your attention for a moment to
the answers which Mr. Lincoln made at Freeport to
the questions which I propounded to him at Ottawa,
based upon the platform adopted by a majority of

the Abolition counties of the State, which now, as then, supported him. In answer to my question whether he indorsed the Black Republican principle of "no more slave States," he answered that he was not pledged against the admission of any more slave States, but that he would be very sorry if he should ever be placed in a position where he would have to vote on the question; that he would rejoice to know that no more slave States would be admitted into the Union.

"But [he added] if slavery shall be kept out of the Territories during the Territorial existence of any one given Territory, and then the people shall, having a fair chance and a clear field when they come to adopt the constitution, do such an extraordinary thing as to adopt a slave constitution, uninfluenced by the actual presence of the institution among them, I see no alternative, if we own the country, but to admit them into the Union."

The point I wish him to answer is this: Suppose Congress should not prohibit slavery in the Territory, and it applied for admission with a constitution recognizing slavery, then how would he vote? His answer at Freeport does not apply to any territory in America. I ask you [turning to Lincoln], will you vote to admit Kansas into the Union, with just such a constitution as her people want, with slavery or without, as they shall determine? He will not answer. I have put that question to him time and time again, and have not been able to get an answer out of him. I ask you again, Lincoln, will you vote to admit New Mexico, when she has the requisite population, with such a constitution as her people adopt, either recognizing slavery or not, as they shall determine? He will not answer. I put the same question to him in reference to Oregon and the new States to be carved out of Texas, in pursuance of the contract between Texas and the United States, and he will not answer. He will not answer these questions in reference to any Territory now in existence, but says that if Congress should prohibit slavery in a Territory, and when its people asked for admission as a State they should adopt slavery as one of their institutions, that he supposes he would have to let it come in. I submit to you whether that answer of his to my question does not justify me in saying that he has a fertile genius in devising language to conceal his thoughts. I ask you whether there is an intelligent man in America who does not believe that that answer was made for the purpose of concealing what he intended to do. He wished to make the old-line Whigs believe that he would stand by the Compromise measures of 1850, which declared that the States might come into the Union with slavery, or without, as they pleased, while Lovejoy and his Abolition allies up north explained to the Abolitionists that in taking this ground he preached good Abolition doctrine, because his proviso would not apply to any Territory in America, and therefore there was no chance of his being governed by it. It would have been quite easy for him to have said that he would let the people of a State do just as they pleased, if he desired to convey

such an idea. Why did he not do it? He would
not answer my question directly, because up north
the Abolition creed declares that there shall be no
more slave States, while down south, in Adams
County, in Coles, and in Sangamon, he and his friends
are afraid to advance that doctrine. Therefore, he
gives an evasive and equivocal answer, to be construed one way in the south and another way in the
north, which, when analyzed, it is apparent is not an
answer at all with reference to any territory now in
existence.

Mr. Lincoln complains that in my speech the other
day at Galesburgh I read an extract from a speech
delivered by him at Chicago, and then another from
his speech at Charleston, and compared them, thus
showing the people that he had one set of principles
in one part of the State, and another in the other part.
And how does he answer that charge? Why, he
quotes from his Charleston speech as I quoted from
it, and then quotes another extract from a speech
which he made at another place, which he says is the
same as the extract from his speech at Charleston;
but he does not quote the extract from his Chicago
speech, upon which I convicted him of double-dealing. I quoted from his Chicago speech to prove that
he held one set of principles up north among the
Abolitionists, and from his Charleston speech to
prove that he held another set down at Charleston
and in southern Illinois. In his answer to this
charge, he ignores entirely his Chicago speech, and
merely argues that he said the same thing which he
said at Charleston at another place. If he did, it

follows that he has twice, instead of once, held one creed in one part of the State, and a different creed in another part. Up at Chicago, in the opening of the campaign, he reviewed my reception speech, and undertook to answer my argument attacking his favorite doctrine of negro equality. I had shown that it was a falsification of the Declaration of Independence to pretend that that instrument applied to and included negroes in the clause declaring that all men were created equal. What was Lincoln's reply? I will read from his Chicago speech and the one which he did not quote, and dare not quote, in this part of the State. He said:

"I should like to know if, taking this old Declaration of Independence, which declares that all men are equal upon principle, and making exceptions to it, where will it stop? If one man says it does not mean a negro, why may not another man say it does not mean another man? If that declaration is not the truth, let us get the statute book in which we find it, and tear it out."

There you find that Mr. Lincoln told the Abolitionists of Chicago that if the Declaration of Independence did not declare that the negro was created by the Almighty the equal of the white man, that you ought to take that instrument and tear out the clause which says that all men were created equal. But let me call your attention to another part of the same speech. You know that in his Charleston speech, an extract from which he has read, he declared that the negro belongs to an inferior race, is physically inferior to the white man, and should always be kept in an inferior position. I will now read to you what he said at Chicago on that point. In concluding his speech at that place, he remarked:

"My friends, I have detained you about as long as I desire to do, and I have only to say, let us discard all this quibbling about this man and the other man, this race, and that race, and the other race being inferior, and therefore they must be placed in an inferior position, discarding our standard that we have left us. Let us discard all these things, and unite as one people throughout this land until we shall once more stand up declaring that all men are created equal."

Thus you see that when addressing the Chicago Abolitionists he declared that all distinctions of race must be discarded and blotted out, because the negro stood on an equal footing with the white man; that if one man said the Declaration of Independence did not mean a negro when it declared all men created equal, that another man would say that it did not mean another man; and hence we ought to discard all differences between the negro race and all other races, and declare them all created equal. Did old Giddings, when he came down among you four years ago, preach more radical Abolitionism than this? Did Lovejoy, or Lloyd Garrison, or Wendell Phillips, or Fred Douglass ever take higher Abolition grounds than that? Lincoln told you that I had charged him with getting up these personal attacks to conceal the enormity of his principles, and then commenced talking about something else, omitting to quote this part of his Chicago speech which contained the enormity of his principles to which I alluded. He knew that I alluded to his negro-equality doctrines when I spoke of the enormity of his principles, yet he did not find it convenient to answer on that point. Having shown you what he said in his Chicago speech in reference to negroes being created equal to white men, and about discarding all distinctions between the two races, I will again read to you what he said at Charleston:

"I will say, then, that I am not nor ever have been in favor of bringing about in any way the social and political equality of the white and black races; that I am not nor ever have been in favor of making voters of the free negroes, or jurors, or qualifying them to hold office, or having them to marry with white people. I will say in addition, that there is a physical difference between the white and black races, which, I suppose, will forever forbid the two races living together upon terms of social and political equality, and inasmuch as they cannot so live, that while they do remain together there must be the position of superior and inferior, that I as much as any other man am in favor of the superior position being assigned to the white man."

A voice: That's the doctrine.

Mr. DOUGLAS: Yes, sir, that is good doctrine; but Mr. Lincoln is afraid to advocate it in the latitude of Chicago, where he hopes to get his votes. It is good doctrine in the anti-Abolition counties for him, and his Chicago speech is good doctrine in the Abolition counties. I assert, on the authority of these two speeches of Mr. Lincoln, that he holds one set of principles in the Abolition counties, and a different and contradictory set in the other counties. I do not question that he said at Ottawa what he quoted; but that only convicts him further, by proving that he has twice contradicted himself, instead of once. Let me ask him why he cannot avow his principles the same in the north as in the south,—the same in every county,—if he has a conviction that they are just? But I forgot,—he would not be a Republican if his principles would apply alike to every part of the country. The party to which he belongs is bounded and limited by geographical lines. With their principles, they cannot even cross the Mississippi River on your ferry-boats. They cannot cross over the Ohio into Kentucky. Lincoln himself cannot visit the land of his fathers, the scenes of his childhood, the graves of his ancestors, and carry his Abolition principles, as he declared them at Chicago, with him.

This Republican organization appeals to the North against the South; it appeals to Northern passion, Northern prejudice, and Northern ambition, against Southern people, Southern States, and Southern institutions, and its only hope of success is by that appeal. Mr. Lincoln goes on to justify himself in making a war upon slavery upon the ground that Frank Blair and Gratz Brown did not succeed in their warfare upon the institution in Missouri. Frank Blair was elected to Congress in 1856, from the State of Missouri, as a Buchanan Democrat, and he turned Fremonter after the people elected him, thus belonging to one party before election, and another afterward. What right then had he to expect, after having thus cheated his constituency, that they would support him at another election? Mr. Lincoln thinks it is his duty to preach a crusade in the free States against slavery, because it is a crime, as he believes, and ought to be extinguished, and because the people of the slave States will never abolish it. How is he going to abolish it? Down in the southern part of the State he takes the ground openly that he will not interfere with slavery where it exists, and says that he is not now and never was in favor of interfering with slavery where it exists in the States. Well, if he is not in favor of that, how does he expect to bring slavery in a course of ultimate extinction? How can he extinguish it in Kentucky, in Virginia, in all the slave States by his policy, if he will not pursue a policy which will interfere with it in the States where it exists? In his speech at Springfield before the Abolition, or Republican, Convention, he declared his hostility to any more slave States in this language:

"Under the operation of that policy the agitation has not only not ceased, but has constantly augmented. In my opinion, it will not cease until a crisis shall have been reached and passed. 'A house divided against itself cannot stand.' I believe this government cannot endure permanently half slave and half free. I do not expect the Union to be dissolved, I do not expect the house to fall; but I do expect it will cease to be divided. It will become all one thing, or all the other. Either the opponents of slavery will arrest the further spread of it, and place it where the public mind shall rest in the belief that it is in the course of ultimate extinction, or its ad-

vocates will push it forward until it shall become alike
lawful in all the States,—old as well as new, North as
well as South."

Mr. Lincoln there told his Abolition friends that
this government could not endure permanently,
divided into free and slave States as our fathers
made it, and that it must become all free or all slave;
otherwise, that the government could not exist.
How then does Lincoln propose to save the Union,
unless by compelling all the States to become free, so
that the house shall not be divided against itself?
He intends making them all free; he will preserve
the Union in that way; and yet he is not going to
interfere with slavery where it now exists.   How is
he going to bring it about?   Why he will agitate, he
will induce the North to agitate, until the South shall
be worried out and forced to abolish slavery.   Let us
examine the policy by which that is to be done.   He
first tells you that he would prohibit slavery everywhere in the Territories.   He would thus confine
slavery within its present limits.   When he thus
gets it confined, and surrounded, so that it cannot
spread, the natural laws of increase will go on until
the negroes will be so plenty that they cannot live on
the soil.   He will hem them in until starvation
seizes them, and by starving them to death he will
put slavery in the course of ultimate extinction.   If
he is not going to interfere with slavery in the States,
but intends to interfere and prohibit it in the Territories, and thus smother slavery out, it naturally follows that he can extinguish it only by extinguishing

the negro race; for his policy would drive them to
starvation. This is the humane and Christian
remedy that he proposes for the great crime of
slavery!

He tells you that I will not argue the question
whether slavery is right or wrong. I tell you why I
will not do it. I hold that, under the Constitution
of the United States, each State of this Union has a
right to do as it pleases on the subject of slavery. In
Illinois we have exercised that sovereign right by
prohibiting slavery within our own limits. I approve
of that line of policy. We have performed our whole
duty in Illinois. We have gone as far as we have a
right to go under the Constitution of our common
country. It is none of our business whether slavery
exists in Missouri or not. Missouri is a sovereign
State of this Union, and has the same right to decide
the slavery question for herself that Illinois has to
decide it for herself. Hence I do not choose to
occupy the time allotted to me in discussing a question that we have no right to act upon. I thought
that you desired to hear us upon those questions
coming within our constitutional power of action.
Lincoln will not discuss these. What one question
has he discussed that comes within the power or
calls for the action or interference of an United States
Senator? He is going to discuss the rightfulness of
slavery when Congress cannot act upon it either way.
He wishes to discuss the merits of the Dred Scott
decision when, under the Constitution, a senator has
no right to interfere with the decision of judicial
tribunals. He wants your exclusive attention to

two questions that he has no power to act upon; to two questions that he could not vote upon if he was in Congress; to two questions that are not practical, —in order to conceal from your attention other questions which he might be required to vote upon should he ever become a member of Congress. He tells you that he does not like the Dred Scott decision. Suppose he does not, how is he going to help himself? He says that he will reverse it. How will he reverse it? I know of but one mode of reversing judicial decisions, and that is by appealing from the inferior to the superior court. But I have never yet learned how or where an appeal could be taken from the Supreme Court of the United States! The Dred Scott decision was pronounced by the highest tribunal on earth. From that decision there is no appeal, this side of heaven. Yet, Mr. Lincoln says he is going to reverse that decision. By what tribunal will he reverse it? Will he appeal to a mob? Does he intend to appeal to violence, to Lynch law? Will he stir up strife and rebellion in the land, and overthrow the court by violence? He does not deign to tell you how he will reverse the Dred Scott decision, but keeps appealing each day from the Supreme Court of the United States to political meetings in the country. He wants me to argue with you the merits of each point of that decision before this political meeting. I say to you, with all due respect, that I choose to abide by the decisions of the Supreme Court as they are pronounced. It is not for me to inquire, after a decision is made, whether I like it in all the points or not. When I used to practise law

with Lincoln, I never knew him to be beat in a case
that he did not get mad at the judge, and talk about
appealing; and when I got beat, I generally thought
the court was wrong, but I never dreamed of going
out of the courthouse and making a stump speech to
the people against the judge, merely because I had
found out that I did not know the law as well as he
did.   If the decision did not suit me, I appealed
until I got to the Supreme Court; and then if that
court, the highest tribunal in the world, decided
against me, I was satisfied, because it is the duty of
every law-abiding man to obey the constitutions,
the laws, and the constituted authorities.   He who
attempts to stir up odium and rebellion in the country against the constituted authorities is stimu-
lating the passions of men to resort to violence and
to mobs instead of to the law.   Hence, I tell you that
I take the decisions of the Supreme Court as the law
of the land, and I intend to obey them as such.

But Mr. Lincoln says that I will not answer his
question as to what I would do in the event of the
court making so ridiculous a decision as he imagines
they would by deciding that the free State of Illinois
could not prohibit slavery within her own limits.   I
told him at Freeport why I would not answer such a
question.   I told him that there was not a man
possessing any brains in America, lawyer or not, who
ever dreamed that such a thing could be done.   I
told him then, as I do now, that by all the principles
set forth in the Dred Scott decision, it is impossible.
I told him then, as I do now, that it is an insult to
men's understanding, and a gross calumny on the

court, to presume in advance that it was going to degrade itself so low as to make a decision known to be in direct violation of the Constitution.

A voice: The same thing was said about the Dred Scott decision before it passed.

Mr. DOUGLAS: Perhaps you think that the court did the same thing in reference to the Dred Scott decision: I have heard a man talk that way before. The principles contained in the Dred Scott decision had been affirmed previously in various other decisions. What court or judge ever held that a negro was a citizen? The State courts had decided that question over and over again, and the Dred Scott decision on that point only affirmed what every court in the land knew to be the law.

But I will not be drawn off into an argument upon the merits of the Dred Scott decision. It is enough for me to know that the Constitution of the United States created the Supreme Court for the purpose of deciding all disputed questions touching the true construction of that instrument, and when such decisions are pronounced, they are the law of the land, binding on every good citizen. Mr. Lincoln has a very convenient mode of arguing upon the subject. He holds that because he is a Republican that he is not bound by the decisions of the court, but that I, being a Democrat, am so bound. It may be that Republicans do not hold themselves bound by the laws of the land and the Constitution of the country as expounded by the courts; it may be an article in the Republican creed that men who do not like a decision have a right to rebel against it: but when

Mr. Lincoln preaches that doctrine, I think he will
find some honest Republican—some law-abiding
man in that party—who will repudiate such a monstrous doctrine. The decision in the Dred Scott
case is binding on every American citizen alike; and
yet Mr. Lincoln argues that the Republicans are not
bound by it because they are opposed to it, whilst
Democrats are bound by it, because we will not resist
it. A Democrat cannot resist the constituted authorities of this country; a Democrat is a law-abiding
man; a Democrat stands by the Constitution and
the laws, and relies upon liberty as protected by
law, and not upon mob or political violence.

I have never yet been able to make Mr. Lincoln
understand, nor can I make any man who is determined to support him, right or wrong, understand
how it is that under the Dred Scott decision the
people of a Territory, as well as a State, can have
slavery or not, just as they please. I believe that I
can explain that proposition to all constitution-lov-
ing, law-abiding men in a way that they cannot fail
to understand it. Chief Justice Taney, in his opinion
in the Dred Scott case, said that, slaves being property, the owner of them has a right to take them into
a Territory the same as he would any other property;
in other words, that slave property, so far as the
right to enter a Territory is concerned, stands on the
same footing with other property. Suppose we
grant that proposition. Then any man has a right to
go to Kansas and take his property with him; but
when he gets there, he must rely upon the local law
to protect his property, whatever it may be. In

order to illustrate this, imagine that three of you
conclude to go to Kansas.   One takes $10,000 worth
of slaves, another $10,000 worth of liquors, and the
third $10,000 worth of dry-goods.   When the man
who owns the dry-goods arrives out there and com-
mences selling them, he finds that he is stopped and
prohibited from selling until he gets a license, to pay
for which will destroy all the profits he can make
on his goods.   When the man with the liquors gets
there and tries to sell, he finds a Maine liquor law in
force which prevents him.   Now, of what use is his
right to go there with his property unless he is protected in the enjoyment of that right after he gets
there?   The man who gets there with his slaves finds
that there is no law to protect him when he arrives
there.   He has no remedy if his slaves run away to
another country; there is no slave code or police
regulations; and the absence of them excludes his
slaves from the Territory just as effectually and as
positively as a constitutional prohibition could.

Such was the understanding when the Kansas and
Nebraska Bill was pending in Congress.   Read the
speech of Speaker Orr, of South Carolina, in the
House of Representatives, in 1856, on the Kansas
question, and you will find that he takes the ground
that while the owner of a slave has a right to go into
a Territory and carry his slaves with him, that he cannot hold them one day or hour unless there is a slave
code to protect him.   He tells you that slavery would
not exist a day in South Carolina, or any other State,
unless there was a friendly people and friendly legislation.   Read the speeches of that giant in intellect,

Alexander H. Stephens, of Georgia, and you will find them to the same effect. Read the speeches of Sam Smith, of Tennessee, and of all Southern men, and you will find that they all understood this doctrine then as we understand it now. Mr. Lincoln cannot be made to understand it, however. Down at Jonesboro, he went on to argue that if it be the law that a man has a right to take his slaves into territory of the United States under the Constitution, that then a member of Congress was perjured if he did not vote for a slave code. I ask him whether the decision of the Supreme Court is not binding upon him as well as on me? If so, and he holds that he would be perjured if he did not vote for a slave code under it, I ask him whether, if elected to Congress, he will so vote? I have a right to his answer, and I will tell you why. He put that question to me down in Egypt, and did it with an air of triumph. This was about the form of it: In the event that a slave-holding citizen of one of the Territories should need and demand a slave code to protect his slaves, will you vote for it? I answered him that a fundamental article in the Democratic creed, as put forth in the Nebraska Bill and the Cincinnati platform, was non-intervention by Congress with slavery in the States and Territories, and hence that I would not vote in Congress for any code of laws either for or against slavery in any Territory. I will leave the people perfectly free to decide that question for themselves.

Mr. Lincoln and the Washington *Union* both think this a monstrous bad doctrine. Neither Mr. Lincoln

nor the Washington *Union* like my Freeport speech
on that subject. The *Union*, in a late number, has
been reading me out of the Democratic party because
I hold that the people of a Territory, like those of a
State, have the right to have slavery or not, as they
please. It has devoted three and a half columns to
prove certain propositions, one of which I will read.
It says:

> "We propose to show that Judge Douglas's action in
> 1850 and 1854 was taken with especial reference to the
> announcement of doctrine and programme which was
> made at Freeport. The declaration at Freeport was
> that 'in his opinion the people can, by lawful means,
> exclude slavery from a Territory before it comes in as a
> State'; and he declared that his competitor had 'heard
> him argue the Nebraska Bill on that principle all over
> Illinois in 1854, 1855, and 1856, and had no excuse to
> pretend to have any doubt upon that subject.' "

The Washington *Union* there charges me with the
monstrous crime of now proclaiming on the stump
the same doctrine that I carried out in 1850, by
supporting Clay's Compromise measures. The *Union*
also charges that I am now proclaiming the same
doctrine that I did in 1854 in support of the Kansas
and Nebraska Bill. It is shocked that I should now
stand where I stood in 1850, when I was supported by
Clay, Webster, Cass, and the great men of that day,
and where I stood in 1854 and in 1856, when Mr.
Buchanan was elected President. It goes on to
prove, and succeeds in proving, from my speeches in
Congress on Clay's Compromise measures, that I

13

held the same doctrines at that time that I do now, and then proves that by the Kansas and Nebraska Bill I advanced the same doctrine that I now advance. It remarks:

"So much for the course taken by Judge Douglas on the Compromises of 1850. The record shows, beyond the possibility of cavil or dispute, that he expressly intended in those bills to give the Territorial Legislatures power to exclude slavery. How stands his record in the memorable session of 1854, with reference to the Kansas-Nebraska Bill itself? We shall not overhaul the votes that were given on that notable measure; our space will not afford it. We have his own words, however, delivered in his speech closing the great debate on that bill on the night of March 3, 1854, to show that *he meant* to do in 1854 precisely what *he had meant* to do in 1858. The Kansas-Nebraska Bill being upon its passage, he said:"

It then quotes my remarks upon the passage of the bill as follows:

"The principle which we propose to carry into effect by this bill is this: That Congress shall neither legislate slavery into any Territory or State, nor out of the same; but the people shall be left free to regulate their domestic concerns in their own way, subject only to the Constitution of the United States. In order to carry this principle into practical operation, it becomes necessary to remove whatever legal obstacles might be found in the way of its free exercise. It is only for the purpose of carrying out this great fundamental principle of self-government that the bill renders the eighth section of the Missouri Act inoperative and void.

"Now, let me ask, will those senators who have ar-

raigned me, or any one of them, have the assurance to
rise in his place and declare that this great principle was
never thought of or advocated as applicable to Territorial bills, in 1850; that, from that session until the
present, nobody ever thought of incorporating this
principle in all new Territorial organizations, etc., etc.?
I will begin with the Compromises of 1850. Any senator
who will take the trouble to examine our journals will
find that on the 25th of March of that year I reported
from the Committee on Territories two bills, including the
following measures: the admission of California, a Territorial government for Utah, a Territorial government for
New Mexico, and the adjustment of the Texas boundary.
These bills proposed to leave the people of Utah and
New Mexico free to decide the slavery question for
themselves, *in the precise language of the Nebraska Bill*
now under discussion. A few weeks afterward the committee of thirteen took those bills and put a wafer between them, and reported them back to the Senate as
one bill, with some slight amendments. *One of these
amendments was, that the Territorial Legislatures should
not legislate upon the subject of African slavery. I objected to this provision,* upon the ground that it sub-
verted the great principle of self-government, *upon
which the bill had been originally framed by the Territorial Committee.* On the first trial the Senate refused
to strike it out, but subsequently did so, upon full debate, in order to establish that principle as the rule of
action in Territorial organizations."

The *Union* comments thus upon my speech on that
occasion:

"Thus it is seen that, in framing the Nebraska-Kansas
Bill, Judge Douglas framed it in the terms and upon the

model of those of Utah and New Mexico, and that in the debate he took pains expressly to revive the recollection of the voting which had taken place upon amendments affecting the powers of the Territorial Legislatures over the subject of slavery in the bills of 1850, in order to give the same meaning, force, and effect to the Nebraska-Kansas Bill on this subject as had been given to those of Utah and New Mexico."

The *Union* proves the following propositions: First, that I sustained Clay's Compromise measures on the ground that they established the principle of self-government in the Territories. Secondly, that I brought in the Kansas and Nebraska Bill, founded upon the same principles as Clay's Compromise measures of 1850; and, thirdly, that my Freeport speech is in exact accordance with those principles. And what do you think is the imputation that the *Union* casts upon me for all this? It says that my Freeport speech is not Democratic, and that I was not a Democrat in 1854 or in 1850! Now is not that funny? Think that the author of the Kansas and Nebraska Bill was not a Democrat when he introduced it! The *Union* says I was not a sound Democrat in 1850, nor in 1854, nor in 1856, nor am I in 1858, because I have always taken and now occupy the ground that the people of a Territory, like those of a State, have the right to decide for themselves whether slavery shall or shall not exist in a Territory! I wish to cite, for the benefit of the Washington *Union* and the followers of that sheet, one authority on that point, and I hope the authority will be deemed satisfactory to that class of politicians. I will read from Mr. Buchanan's letter accepting the nomination of the Democratic Convention, for the Presidency. You know that Mr. Buchanan, after he was nominated, declared to the Keystone Club, in a public speech, that he was no longer James Buchanan but the embodiment of the Democratic platform. In his letter to the committee which informed him of his nomination, accepting it, he defined the meaning of the Kansas and Nebraska Bill and the Cincinnati platform in these words:

"The recent legislation of Congress respecting domestic slavery, derived as it has been from the original and pure fountain of legitimate political power, the will of the majority, promises ere long to allay the dangerous excitement. This legislation is founded upon principles as ancient as free government itself, and, in accordance with them, has simply declared that the people of a Territory, like those of a State, shall decide for themselves whether slavery shall or shall not exist within their limits."

Thus you see that James Buchanan accepted the nomination at Cincinnati on the condition that the people of a Territory, like those of a State, should be left to decide for themselves whether slavery should or should not exist within their limits. I sustained James Buchanan for the Presidency on that platform as adopted at Cincinnati, and expounded by himself. He was elected President on that platform, and now we are told by the Washington *Union* that no man is a true Democrat who stands on the platform on which Mr. Buchanan was nominated, and which he has explained and expounded himself.

We are told that a man is not a Democrat who stands by Clay, Webster, and Cass, and the Compromise measures of 1850, and the Kansas and Nebraska Bill of 1854. Whether a man be a Democrat or not on that platform, I intend to stand there as long as I have life. I intend to cling firmly to that principle which declares the right of each State and each Territory to settle the question of slavery, and every other domestic question, for themselves. I hold that if they want a slave State they have a right under the Constitution of the United States to make it so, and if they want a free State, it is their right to have it. But the *Union*, in advocating the claims of Lincoln over me to the Senate, lays down two un-pardonable heresies which it says I advocate. The first is the right of the people of a Territory, the same as a State, to decide for themselves the question whether slavery shall exist within their limits, in the language of Mr. Buchanan; and the second is, that a constitution shall be submitted to the people of a Territory for its adoption or rejection before their admission as a State under it. It so happens that Mr. Buchanan is pledged to both these heresies, for supporting which the Washington *Union* has read me out of the Democratic church. In his annual message he said he trusted that the example of the Minnesota case would be followed in all future cases, requiring a submission of the constitution; and in his letter of acceptance, he said that the people of a Territory, the same as a State, had the right to de-cide for themselves whether slavery should exist within their limits. Thus you find that this little

corrupt gang who control the *Union* and wish to
elect Lincoln in preference to me,—because, as they
say, of these two heresies which I support,—denounce
President Buchanan when they denounce me, if he
stands now by the principles on which he was elected.
Will they pretend that he does not now stand by the
principles on which he was elected?   Do they hold
that he has abandoned the Kansas-Nebraska Bill,
the Cincinnati platform, and his own letter accepting
his nomination, all of which declare the right of the
people of a Territory, the same as a State, to decide
the slavery question for themselves?   I will not
believe that he has betrayed or intends to betray
the platform which elected him, but if he does I will
not follow him.   I will stand by that great principle
no matter who may desert it.   I intend to stand by
it, for the purpose of preserving peace between the
North and the South, the free and the slave States.
If each State will only agree to mind its own business
and let its neighbors alone, there will be peace forever
between us.

We in Illinois tried slavery when a Territory, and
found it was not good for us in this climate, and with
our surroundings, and hence we abolished it.   We
then adopted a free State constitution, as we had a
right to do.   In this State we have declared that a
negro shall not be a citizen, and we have also declared that he shall not be a slave.   We had a right
to adopt that policy.   Missouri has just as good a
right to adopt the other policy.   I am now speaking
of rights under the Constitution, and not of moral or
religious rights.   I do not discuss the morals of the

people of Missouri, but let them settle that matter for themselves. I hold that the people of the slave-holding States are civilized men as well as ourselves, that they bear consciences as well as we, and that they are accountable to God and their posterity, and not to us. It is for them to decide, therefore, the moral and religious right of the slavery question for themselves, within their own limits. I assert that they had as much right under the Constitution to adopt the system of policy which they have as we had to adopt ours. So it is with every other State in this Union. Let each State stand firmly by that great constitutional right, let each State mind its own business and let its neighbors alone, and there will be no trouble on this question. If we will stand by that principle, then Mr. Lincoln will find that this Republic can exist forever divided into free and slave States, as our fathers made it and the people of each State have decided. Stand by that great principle, and we can go on as we have been, increasing in wealth, in population, in power, and in all the elements of greatness, until we shall be the admiration and terror of the world. We can go on and enlarge as our population increases and requires more room, until we make this continent one ocean-bound republic. Under that principle the United States can perform that great mission, that destiny, which Providence has marked out for us. Under that principle we can receive with entire safety that stream of intelligence which is constantly flowing from the Old World to the New, filling up our prairies, clearing our wildernesses, and building cities, towns, railroads, and other internal improvements, and thus make this the asylum of the oppressed of the whole earth. We have this great mission to perform, and it can only be performed by adhering faithfully to that principle of self-government on which our institutions were all established. I repeat that the principle is the right of each State, each Territory, to decide this slavery question for itself, to have slavery or not, as it chooses; and it does not become Mr. Lincoln, or anybody else, to tell the people of Kentucky that they have no consciences, that they are living in a state of iniquity, and that they are cherishing an institution to their bosoms in violation of the law of God. Better for him to adopt the doctrine of "Judge not, lest ye shall be judged." Let him perform his own duty at home, and he will have a better fate in the future. I think there are objects of charity enough in the free States to excite the sympathies and open the pockets of all the benevolence we have amongst us, without going abroad in search of negroes, of whose condition we know nothing. We have enough objects of charity at home, and it is our duty to take care of our own poor and our own suffering, before we go abroad to intermeddle with other people's business.

My friends, I am told that my time is within two minutes of expiring. I have omitted many topics that I would like to have discussed before you at length. There were many points touched by Mr. Lincoln that I have not been able to take up for the want of time. I have hurried over each subject that I have discussed as rapidly as possible, so as to omit but few; but one hour and a half is not time sufficient for a man to discuss at length one half of the great questions which are now dividing the public mind.

In conclusion, I desire to return to you my grateful acknowledgments for the kindness and the courtesy with which you have listened to me. It is something remarkable that in an audience as vast as this, composed of men of opposite politics and views, with their passions highly excited, there should be so much courtesy, kindness, and respect exhibited, not only toward one another, but toward the speakers; and I feel that it is due to you that I should thus express my gratitude for the kindness with which you have treated me.

MR. LINCOLN'S REJOINDER.

MY FRIENDS: Since Judge Douglas has said to you in his conclusion that he had not time in an hour and a half to answer all I had said in an hour, it follows of course that I will not be able to answer in half an hour all that he said in an hour and a half.

I wish to return to Judge Douglas my profound thanks for his public annunciation here to-day, to be put on record, that his system of policy in regard to the institution of slavery *contemplates that it shall last forever*. We are getting a little nearer the true issue of this controversy, and I am profoundly grateful for this one sentence. Judge Douglas asks you, Why cannot the institution of slavery, or rather, why cannot the nation, part slave and part free, continue as our fathers made it, *forever?* In the first place, I insist that our fathers *did not* make this nation half slave and half free, or part slave and part free. I insist that they found the institution of slavery existing here. They did not make it so but they left it so because they knew of no way to get rid of it at that time. When Judge Douglas undertakes to say that, as a matter of choice, the fathers of the government made this nation part slave and part free, *he assumes what is historically a falsehood.* More than that: when the fathers of the government cut off the source of slavery by the abolition of the slave-trade, and adopted a system of restricting it from the new Territories where it had not existed, I maintain that they placed it where they understood, and all sensible men understood, it was in the course of ultimate extinction; and when Judge Douglas asks me why it cannot continue as our fathers made it, I ask him why he and his friends could not let it remain as our fathers made it?

It is precisely all I ask of him in relation to the institution of slavery, that it shall be placed upon the basis that our fathers placed it upon. Mr. Brooks, of South Carolina, once said, and truly said, that when this government was established, no one expected the institution of slavery to last until this day, and that the men who formed this government were wiser and better than the men of these days; but the men of these days had experience which the fathers had not, and that experience had taught them the invention of the cotton-gin, and this had made the perpetuation of the institution of slavery a necessity

in this country. Judge Douglas could not let it
stand upon the basis which our fathers placed it, but
removed it, and *put it upon the cotton-gin basis.*   It is
a question, therefore, for him and his friends to
answer, why they could not let it remain where the
fathers of the government originally placed it.

I hope nobody has understood me as trying to
sustain the doctrine that we have a right to quarrel
with Kentucky, or Virginia, or any of the slave
States, about the institution of slavery,—thus giving
the Judge an opportunity to be eloquent and valiant
against us in fighting for their rights.   I expressly
declared in my opening speech that I had neither
the inclination to exercise, nor the belief in the existence of, the right to interfere with the States of
Kentucky or Virginia in doing as they pleased with
slavery or any other existing institution.   Then
what becomes of all his eloquence in behalf of the
rights of States, which are assailed by no living man?

But I have to hurry on, for I have but a half hour.
The Judge has informed me, or informed this audience, that the Washington *Union* is laboring for my
election to the United States Senate.   This is news to
me,—not very ungrateful news either.   [Turning to
Mr. W. H. Carlin, who was on the stand]—I hope
that Carlin will be elected to the State Senate, and
will vote for me.   [Mr. Carlin shook his head.]
Carlin don't fall in, I perceive, and I suppose he will
not do much for me; but I am glad of all the support
I can get, anywhere, if I can get it without practising
any deception to obtain it.   In respect to this large
portion of Judge Douglas's speech in which he tries to

show that in the controversy between himself and the Administration party he is in the right, I do not feel myself at all competent or inclined to answer him. I say to him, "Give it to them,—give it to them just all you can!" and, on the other hand, I say to Carlin, and Jake Davis, and to this man Wogley up here in Hancock, "Give it to Douglas,— just pour it into him!"

Now, in regard to this matter of the Dred Scott decision, I wish to say a word or two. After all, the Judge will not say whether, if a decision is made holding that the people of the *States* cannot exclude slavery, he will support it or not. He obstinately refuses to say what he will do in that case. The judges of the Supreme Court as obstinately refused to say what they would do on this subject. Before this I reminded him that at Galesburgh he said the judges had expressly declared the contrary, and you remember that in my opening speech I told him I had the book containing that decision here, and I would thank him to lay his finger on the place where any such thing was said. He has occupied his hour and a half, and he has not ventured to try to sustain his assertion. *He never will.* But he is desirous of knowing how we are going to reverse that Dred Scott decision. Judge Douglas ought to know how. Did not he and his political friends find a way to reverse the decision of that same court in favor of the constitutionality of the National Bank? Did n't they find a way to do it so effectually that they have reversed it as completely as any decision ever was reversed, so far as its practical operation is concerned?

And let me ask you, did n't Judge Douglas find a way to reverse the decision of our Supreme Court when it decided that Carlin's father—old Governor Carlin—had not the constitutional power to remove a Secretary of State? Did he not appeal to the "MOBS," as he calls them? Did he not make speeches in the lobby to show how villainous that decision was, and how it ought to be overthrown? Did he not succeed, too, in getting an act passed by the Legislature to have it overthrown? And did n't he himself sit down on that bench as one of the five added judges, who were to overslaugh the four old ones,—getting his name of "Judge" in that way, and no other? If there is a villainy in using disrespect or making opposition to Supreme Court decisions, I commend it to Judge Douglas's earnest consideration. I know of no man in the State of Illinois who ought to know so well about *how much* villainy it takes to oppose a decision of the Supreme Court as our honorable friend Stephen A. Douglas.

Judge Douglas also makes the declaration that I say the Democrats are bound by the Dred Scott decision, while the Republicans are not. In the sense in which he argues, I never said it; but I will tell you what I have said and what I do not hesitate to repeat to-day. I have said that as the Democrats believe that decision to be correct, and that the extension of slavery is affirmed in the National Constitution, they are bound to support it as such; and I will tell you here that General Jackson once said each man was bound to support the Constitution "as he understood it." Now, Judge Douglas understands the Constitution according to the Dred Scott decision, and he is bound to support it as he understands it. I understand it another way, and therefore I am bound to support it in the way in which I understand it. And as Judge Douglas believes that decision to be correct, I will remake that argument if I have time to do so. Let me talk to some gentleman down there among you who looks me in the face. We will say you are a member of the Territorial Legislature, and, like Judge Douglas, you believe that the right to take and hold slaves there is a constitutional right. The first thing you do is to *swear you will support the Constitution* and all rights guaranteed therein; that you will, whenever your neighbor needs your legislation to support his constitutional rights, not withhold that legislation. If you withhold that necessary legislation for the support of the Constitution and constitutional rights, do you not commit perjury? I ask every sensible man if that is not so? That is undoubtedly just so, say what you please. Now, that is precisely what Judge Douglas says, that this is a constitutional right. Does the Judge mean to say that the Territorial Legislature in legislating may, by withholding necessary laws, or by passing unfriendly laws, *nullify that constitutional right?* Does he mean to say that? Does he mean to ignore the proposition so long and well established in law, that what you cannot do directly, you cannot do indirectly? Does he mean that? The truth about the matter is this: Judge Douglas has sung pæans to his "Popular Sovereignty" doctrine until his Supreme Court, co-operating with

him, has *squatted* his Squatter Sovereignty out.
But he will keep up this species of humbuggery
about Squatter Sovereignty. He has at last invented this sort of *do-nothing sovereignty*,—that the
people may exclude slavery by a sort of "sovereignty" that is exercised by doing nothing at all.
Is not that running his Popular Sovereignty down
awfully? Has it not got down as thin as the homœo-
pathic soup that was made by boiling the shadow of
a pigeon that had starved to death? But at last,
when it is brought to the test of close reasoning, there
is not even that thin decoction of it left. It is a
presumption impossible in the domain of thought.
It is precisely no other than the putting of that most
unphilosophical proposition, that two bodies can
occupy the same space at the same time. The Dred
Scott decision covers the whole ground, and while
it occupies it, there is no room even for the shadow of
a starved pigeon to occupy the same ground.

Judge Douglas, in reply to what I have said about
having upon a previous occasion made the speech at
Ottawa as the one he took an extract from at Charleston, says it only shows that I practised the deception
twice. Now, my friends, are any of you obtuse
enough to swallow that? Judge Douglas had said I
had made a speech at Charleston that I would not
make up north, and I turned around and answered
him by showing I *had* made that same speech up
north,—had made it at Ottawa; made it in his hearing; made it in *the* Abolition District,—in Lovejoy's
District,—in the personal presence of Lovejoy himself,—in the same atmosphere exactly in which I

had made my Chicago speech, of which he complains so much.

Now, in relation to my not having said anything about the quotation from the Chicago speech: he thinks that is a terrible subject for me to handle. Why, gentlemen, I can show you that the substance of the Chicago speech I delivered two years ago in "Egypt," as he calls it. It was down at Springfield. That speech is here in this book, and I could turn to it and read it to you but for the lack of time. I have not now the time to read it. ["Read it, read it."] No, gentlemen, I am obliged to use discretion in disposing most advantageously of my brief time. The Judge has taken great exception to my adopting the heretical statement in the Declaration of Independence, that "all men are created equal," and he has a great deal to say about negro equality. I want to say that in sometimes alluding to the Declaration of Independence, I have only uttered the sentiments that Henry Clay used to hold. Allow me to occupy your time a moment with what he said. Mr. Clay was at one time called upon in Indiana, and in a way that I suppose was very insulting, to liberate his slaves; and he made a written reply to that application, and one portion of it is in these words:

"What is the *foundation* of this appeal to me in Indiana to liberate the slaves under my care in Kentucky? It is a general declaration in the act announcing to the world the independence of the thirteen American colonies, that '*men are created equal*.' Now, as an abstract principle, *there is no doubt of the truth of that declaration*, and it is desirable in the *original construction* of society, and

14

in organized societies, to keep it in view as a great fundamental principle.''

When I sometimes, in relation to the organization
of new societies in new countries, where the soil is
clean and clear, insisted that we should keep that
principle in view, Judge Douglas will have it that I
want a negro wife. He never can be brought to
understand that there is any middle ground on this
subject. I have lived until my fiftieth year, and
have never had a negro woman either for a slave or a
wife, and I think I can live fifty centuries, for that
matter, without having had one for either. I maintain that you may take Judge Douglas's quotations
from my Chicago speech, and from my Charleston
speech, and the Galesburgh speech,—in his speech
of to-day,—and compare them over, and I am willing to trust them with you upon his proposition that
they show rascality or double-dealing. I deny that
they do.

The Judge does not seem at all disposed to have
peace, but I find he is disposed to have a personal
warfare with me. He says that my oath would not
be taken against the bare word of Charles H. Lanphier or Thomas L. Harris. Well, that is altogether
a matter of opinion. It is certainly not for me to
vaunt my word against oaths of these gentlemen,
but I will tell Judge Douglas again the facts upon
which I "*dared*" to say they proved a forgery. I
pointed out at Galesburgh that the publication of
these resolutions in the Illinois *State Register* could
not have been the result of accident, as the proceed-

ings of that meeting bore unmistakable evidence of
being done by a man who *knew* it was a forgery;
that it was a publication partly taken from the real
proceedings of the Convention, and partly from the
proceedings of a convention at another place,—
which showed that he had the real proceedings before him, and taking one part of the resolutions, he
threw out another part, and substituted false and
fraudulent ones in their stead. I pointed that out to
him, and also that his friend Lanphier, who was
editor of the *Register* at that time and now is, must
have known how it was done. Now, whether *he*
did it, or got some friend to do it for him, I could
not tell, but he certainly knew all about it. I
pointed out to Judge Douglas that in his Freeport
speech he had promised to *investigate* that matter.
Does he now say he did not make that promise? I
have a right to ask *why he did not keep it*. I call
upon him to tell here to-day why he did not keep
that promise? That fraud has been traced up so
that it lies between him, Harris, and Lanphier.
There is little room for escape for Lanphier. Lanphier is doing the Judge good service, and Douglas
desires his word to be taken for the truth. He
desires Lanphier to be taken as authority in what
he states in his newspaper. He desires Harris to be
taken as a man of vast credibility; and when this
thing lies among them, they will not press it to show
where the guilt really belongs. Now, as he has said
that he would investigate it, and implied that he
would tell us the result of his investigation, I demand of him to tell why he did not investigate it,

if he did not; and if he did, *why he won't tell the result.* I call upon him for that.

This is the third time that Judge Douglas has assumed that he learned about these resolutions by Harris's attempting to use them against Norton on the floor of Congress. I tell Judge Douglas the public records of the country show that *he* himself attempted it upon Trumbull a month before Harris tried them on Norton; that Harris had the opportunity of *learning it from him*, rather than he from Harris. I now ask his attention to that part of the record on the case. My friends, I am not disposed to detain you longer in regard to that matter.

I am told that I still have five minutes left. There is another matter I wish to call attention to. He says, when he discovered there was a mistake in that case, he came forward magnanimously, without my calling his attention to it, and explained it. I will tell you how he became so magnanimous. When the newspapers of our side had discovered and published it, and put it beyond his power to deny it, then he came forward and made a virtue of necessity by acknowledging it. Now he argues that all the point there was in those resolutions, although never passed at Springfield, is retained by their being passed at other localities. Is that true? He said I had a hand in passing them, in his opening speech,— that I was in the convention and helped to pass them. Do the resolutions touch me at all? It strikes me there is some difference between holding a man responsible for an act which he *has not* done and holding him responsible for an act that he *has* done. You will judge whether there is any difference in the "*spots.*" And he has taken credit for great magnanimity in coming forward and acknowledging what is proved on him beyond even the capacity of Judge Douglas to deny; and he has more capacity in that way than any other living man.

Then he wants to know why I won't withdraw the charge in regard to a conspiracy to make slavery national, as he has withdrawn the one he made. May it please his worship, I will withdraw it *when it is proven false on me as that was proven false on him.* I will add a little more than that. I will withdraw it whenever a reasonable man shall be brought to believe that the charge is not true. I have asked Judge Douglas's attention to certain matters of fact tending to prove the charge of a conspiracy to nationalize slavery, and he says he convinces me that this is all untrue because Buchanan was not in the country at that time, and because the Dred Scott case had not then got into the Supreme Court; and he says that I say the *Democratic* owners of Dred Scott got up the case. I never did say that. I defy Judge Douglas to show that I ever said so, *for I never uttered it.* [One of Mr. Douglas's reporters gesticulated affirmatively at Mr. Lincoln.] I don't care if your hireling does say I did, I tell you myself that *I never said the "Democratic" owners of Dred Scott got up the case.* I have never pretended to know whether Dred Scott's owners were Democrats, or Abolitionists, or Free-soilers or Border Ruffians. I have said that there is evidence about the case tending to show that it was a made-up case, for the purpose of getting that decision. I have said that that evidence was very strong in the fact that when Dred Scott was declared to be a slave, the owner of him made him free, showing that he had had the case tried and the question settled for such use as could be made of that decision; he cared nothing about the property thus declared to be his by that decision. But my time is out, and I can say no more.

THE LAST JOINT DEBATE, AT ALTON,

OCTOBER 15, 1858.

SENATOR DOUGLAS'S SPEECH.

LADIES AND GENTLEMEN: It is now nearly four months since the canvass between Mr. Lincoln and myself commenced. On the 16th of June the Republican Convention assembled at Springfield and nominated Mr. Lincoln as their candidate for the United States Senate, and he, on that occasion, delivered a speech in which he laid down what he understood to be the Republican creed, and the platform on which he proposed to stand during the contest. The principal points in that speech of Mr. Lincoln's were: First, that this government could not endure permanently divided into free and slave States, as our fathers made it; that they must all become free or all become slave; all become one thing, or all become the other,—otherwise this Union could not continue to exist. I give you his opinions almost in the identical language he used. His second proposition was a crusade against the Supreme Court of the United States because of the Dred Scott decision, urging as an especial reason for his opposition to that decision that it deprived the negroes of the rights and benefits of that clause in the Constitution of the United States which guarantees to the citizens of each State all the rights, privileges, and immunities of the citizens of the several States.   On the 10th of July I returned home, and delivered a speech to the people of Chicago, in which I announced it to be my purpose to appeal to the people of Illinois to sustain the course I had pursued in Congress.   In that speech I joined issue with Mr. Lincoln on the points which he had presented.   Thus there was an issue clear and distinct made up between us on these two propositions laid down in the speech of Mr. Lincoln at Springfield, and controverted by me in my reply to him at Chicago.   On the next day, the 11th of July, Mr. Lincoln replied to me at Chicago, explaining at some length and reaffirming the positions which he had taken in his Springfield speech.   In that Chicago speech he even went further than he had before, and uttered sentiments in regard to the negro being on an equality with the white man.   He adopted in support of this position the argument which Lovejoy and Codding and other Abolition lecturers had made familiar in the northern and central portions of the State: to wit, that the Declaration of Independence having declared all men free and equal, by divine law, also that negro equality was an inalienable right, of which they could not be deprived.   He insisted, in that speech, that the Declaration of Independence included the negro in the clause asserting that all men were created equal, and went so far as to say that if one man was allowed to take the position that it did not include the negro, others might take the position that it did not include other men.   He said that all these distinctions between this man and that man, this race and the other race, must be discarded, and we must all stand by the Declaration of Independence, declaring that all men were created equal.

The issue thus being made up between Mr. Lincoln and myself on three points, we went before the people of the State. During the following seven weeks, between the Chicago speeches and our first meeting at Ottawa, he and I addressed large assemblages of the people in many of the central counties. In my speeches I confined myself closely to those three positions which he had taken, controverting his proposition that this Union could not exist as our fathers made it, divided into free and slave States, controverting his proposition of a crusade against the Supreme Court because of the Dred Scott decision, and controverting his proposition that the Declaration of Independence included and meant the negroes as well as the white men, when it declared all men to be created equal. I supposed at that time that these propositions constituted a distinct issue between us, and that the opposite positions we had taken upon them we would be willing to be held to in every part of the State. I never intended to waver one hair's breadth from that issue either in the north or the south, or wherever I should address the people of Illinois. I hold that when the time arrives that I cannot proclaim my political creed in the same terms, not only in the northern, but the southern part of Illinois, not only in the Northern, but the Southern States, and wherever the American flag waves over American soil, that then there must be something wrong in that creed; so long as we live under a common Constitution, so long as we live in a confederacy of sovereign and equal States, joined together as one for certain purposes, that any political creed is radically wrong which cannot be proclaimed in every State and every section of that Union, alike. I took up Mr. Lincoln's three propositions in my several speeches, analyzed them, and pointed out what I believed to be the radical errors contained in them. First, in regard to his doctrine that this government was in violation of the law of God, which says that a house divided against itself cannot stand, I repudiated it as a slander upon the immortal framers of our Constitution. I then said, I have often repeated, and now again assert, that in my opinion our government can endure forever, divided into free and slave States as our fathers made it,—each State having the right to prohibit, abolish, or sustain slavery, just as it pleases. This government was made upon the great basis of the sovereignty of the States, the right of each State to regulate its own domestic institutions to suit itself; and that right was conferred with the understanding and expectation that, inasmuch as each locality had separate interests, each locality must have different and distinct local and domestic institutions, corresponding to its wants and interests. Our fathers knew when they made the government that the laws and institutions which were well adapted to the Green Mountains of Vermont were unsuited to the rice plantations of South Carolina. They knew then, as well as we know now, that the laws and in-

stitutions which would be well adapted to the
beautiful prairies of Illinois would not be suited to
the mining regions of California. They knew that
in a republic as broad as this, having such a variety
of soil, climate, and interest, there must necessarily
be a corresponding variety of local laws,—the policy
and institutions of each State adapted to its condition and wants. For this reason this Union was
established on the right of each State to do as it
pleased on the question of slavery, and every other
question; and the various States were not allowed
to complain of, much less interfere with, the policy
of their neighbors.

Suppose the doctrine advocated by Mr. Lincoln
and the Abolitionists of this day had prevailed when
the Constitution was made, what would have been
the result? Imagine for a moment that Mr. Lincoln
had been a member of the Convention that framed
the Constitution of the United States, and that
when its members were about to sign that wonderful
document, he had arisen in that Convention as he
did at Springfield this summer, and, addressing himself to the President, had said: "A house divided
against itself cannot stand; this government divided
into free and slave States cannot endure, they must
all be free or all be slave; they must all be one thing,
or all the other, otherwise, it is a violation of the
law of God, and cannot continue to exist";—suppose
Mr. Lincoln had convinced that body of sages that
that doctrine was sound, what would have been
the result? Remember that the Union was then
composed of thirteen States, twelve of which were

slaveholding, and one free. Do you think that the one free State would have outvoted the twelve slaveholding States, and thus have secured the abolition of slavery? On the other hand, would not the twelve slaveholding States have outvoted the one free State, and thus have fastened slavery, by a constitutional provision, on every foot of the American Republic forever? You see that if this Abolition doctrine of Mr. Lincoln had prevailed when the government was made, it would have established slavery as a permanent institution in all the States, whether they wanted it or not; and the question for us to determine in Illinois now, as one of the free States, is whether or not we are willing, having become the majority section, to enforce a doctrine on the minority which we would have resisted with our heart's blood had it been attempted on us when we were in a minority. How has the South lost her power as the majority section in this Union, and how have the free States gained it, except under the operation of that principle which declares the right of the people of each State and each Territory to form and regulate their domestic institutions in their own way? It was under that principle that slavery was abolished in New Hampshire, Rhode Island, Connecticut, New York, New Jersey, and Pennsylvania; it was under that principle that one half of the slaveholding States became free; it was under that principle that the number of free States increased until, from being one out of twelve States, we have grown to be the majority of States of the whole Union, with the power to control the House of Representatives and Senate, and the power, consequently, to elect a President by Northern votes, without the aid of a Southern State. Having obtained this power under the operation of that great principle, are you now prepared to abandon the principle and declare that merely because we have the power you will wage a war against the Southern States and their institutions until you force them to abolish slavery everywhere?

After having pressed these arguments home on Mr. Lincoln for seven weeks, publishing a number of my speeches, we met at Ottawa in joint discussion, and he then began to crawfish a little, and let himself down. I there propounded certain questions to him. Amongst others, I asked him whether he would vote for the admission of any more slave States, in the event the people wanted them. He would not answer. I then told him that if he did not answer the question there, I would renew it at Freeport, and would then trot him down into Egypt, and again put it to him. Well, at Freeport, knowing that the next joint discussion took place in Egypt, and being in dread of it, he did answer my question in regard to no more slave States in a mode which he hoped would be satisfactory to me, and accomplish the object he had in view. I will show you what his answer was. After saying that he was not pledged to the Republican doctrine of "no more slave States," he declared:

"I state to you freely, frankly, that I should be exceedingly sorry to ever be put in the position of having to pass upon that question. I should be exceedingly glad to know that there never would be another slave State admitted into this Union."

Here permit me to remark, that I do not think the people will ever force him into a position against his will. He went on to say:

"But I must add, in regard to this, that if slavery shall be kept out of the Territory during the Territorial existence of any one given Territory, and then the people should, having a fair chance and a clear field, when they come to adopt a constitution, if they should do the extraordinary thing of adopting a slave constitution uninfluenced by the actual presence of the institution among them, I see no alternative, if we own the country, but we must admit it into the Union."

That answer Mr. Lincoln supposed would satisfy the old-line Whigs, composed of Kentuckians and Virginians, down in the southern part of the State. Now, what does it amount to? I desired to know whether he would vote to allow Kansas to come into the Union with slavery or not, as her people desired. He would not answer, but in a roundabout way said that if slavery should be kept out of a Territory during the whole of its Territorial existence, and then the people, when they adopted a State Constitution, asked admission as a slave State, he supposed he would have to let the State come in. The case I put to him was an entirely different one. I desired to know whether he would vote to admit a State if Congress had not prohibited slavery in it during its

Territorial existence, as Congress never pretended to do under Clay's Compromise measures of 1850. He would not answer, and I have not yet been able to get an answer from him. I have asked him whether he would vote to admit Nebraska if her people asked to come in as a State with a constitution recognizing slavery, and he refused to answer. I have put the question to him with reference to New Mexico, and he has not uttered a word in answer. I have enumerated the Territories, one after another, putting the same question to him with reference to each, and he has not said, and will not say, whether, if elected to Congress, he will vote to admit any Territory now in existence with such a constitution as her people may adopt. He invents a case which does not exist, and cannot exist under this government, and answers it; but he will not answer the question I put to him in connection with any of the Territories now in existence. The contract we entered into with Texas when she entered the Union obliges us to allow four States to be formed out of the old State, and admitted with or without slavery, as the respective inhabitants of each may determine. I have asked Mr. Lincoln three times in our joint discussions whether he would vote to redeem that pledge, and he has never yet answered. He is as silent as the grave on the subject. He would rather answer as to a state of the case which will never arise than commit himself by telling what he would do in a case which would come up for his action soon after his election to Congress. Why can he not say whether he is willing to allow the people of each

State to have slavery or not as they please, and to come into the Union, when they have the requisite population, as a slave or a free State as they decide? I have no trouble in answering the question. I have said everywhere, and now repeat it to you, that if the people of Kansas want a slave State they have a right, under the Constitution of the United States, to form such a State, and I will let them come into the Union with slavery or without, as they determine. If the people of any other Territory desire slavery, let them have it. If they do not want it, let them prohibit it. It is their business, not mine. It is none of our business in Illinois whether Kansas is a free State or a slave State. It is none of your business in Missouri whether Kansas shall adopt slavery or reject it. It is the business of her people, and none of yours. The people of Kansas have as much right to decide that question for themselves as you have in Missouri to decide it for yourselves, or we in Illinois to decide it for ourselves.

And here I may repeat what I have said in every speech I have made in Illinois, that I fought the Lecompton Constitution to its death not because of the slavery clause in it, but because it was not the act and deed of the people of Kansas. I said then in Congress, and I say now, that if the people of Kansas want a slave State, they have a right to have it. If they wanted the Lecompton Constitution, they had a right to have it. I was opposed to that constitution because I did not believe that it was the act and deed of the people, but, on the contrary, the act of a small, pitiful minority acting in the name of the majority. When at last it was determined to send that constitution back to the people, and, accordingly, in August last, the question of admission under it was submitted to a popular vote, the citizens rejected it by nearly ten to one, thus showing conclusively that I was right when I said that the Lecompton Constitution was not the act and deed of the people of Kansas, and did not embody their will.

I hold that there is no power on earth, under our system of government, which has the right to force a constitution upon an unwilling people. Suppose that there had been a majority of ten to one in favor of slavery in Kansas, and suppose there had been an Abolition President and an Abolition Administration, and by some means the Abolitionists succeeded in forcing an Abolition constitution upon those slaveholding people, would the people of the South have submitted to that act for an instant? Well, if you of the South would not have submitted to it a day, how can you, as fair, honorable, and honest men, insist on putting a slave constitution on a people who desire a free State? Your safety and ours depend upon both of us acting in good faith, and living up to that great principle which asserts the right of every people to form and regulate their domestic institutions to suit themselves, subject only to the Constitution of the United States.

Most of the men who denounced my course on the Lecompton question objected to it, not because I was not right, but because they thought it expedient at that time, for the sake of keeping the party together, to do wrong. I never knew the Democratic party to violate any one of its principles, out of policy or expediency, that it did not pay the debt with sorrow. There is no safety or success for our party unless we always do right, and trust the consequences to God and the people. I chose not to depart from principle for the sake of expediency on the Lecompton question, and I never intend to do it on that or any other question.

But I am told that I would have been all right if I had only voted for the English bill after Lecompton was killed. You know a general pardon was granted to all political offenders on the Lecompton question, provided they would only vote for the English bill. I did not accept the benefits of that pardon, for the reason that I had been right in the course I had pursued, and hence did not require any forgiveness. Let us see how the result has been worked out. English brought in his bill referring the Lecompton Constitution back to the people, with the provision that if it was rejected, Kansas should be kept out of the Union until she had the full ratio of population required for a member of Congress,—thus in effect declaring that if the people of Kansas would only consent to come into the Union under the Lecompton Constitution, and have a slave State when they did not want it, they should be admitted with a population of 35,000; but that if they were so obstinate as to insist upon having just such a constitution as they thought best, and to desire admission as a free State, then they should be kept out until they had 93,420 inhabitants. I then said, and I now repeat to you, that whenever Kansas has people enough for a slave State she has people enough for a free State. I was and am willing to adopt the rule that no State shall ever come into the Union until she has the full ratio of population for a member of Congress, provided that rule is made uniform. I made that proposition in the Senate last winter, but a majority of the senators would not agree to it; and I then said to them, If you will not adopt the general rule, I will not consent to make an exception of Kansas.

I hold that it is a violation of the fundamental principles of this government to throw the weight of Federal power into the scale, either in favor of the free or the slave States. Equality among all the States of this Union is a fundamental principle in our political system. We have no more right to throw the weight of the Federal Government into the scale in favor of the slaveholding than the free States, and least of all should our friends in the South consent for a moment that Congress should withhold its powers either way when they know that there is a majority against them in both Houses of Congress.

Fellow-citizens, how have the supporters of the English bill stood up to their pledges not to admit Kansas until she obtained a population of 93,420 in the event she rejected the Lecompton Constitution? How? The newspapers inform us that English himself, whilst conducting his canvass for re-election, and in order to secure it, pledged himself to his constituents that if returned he would disregard his own bill and vote to admit Kansas into the Union with such population as she might have when she made application. We are informed that every Democratic candidate for Congress in all the States where elections have recently been held was pledged against the English bill, with perhaps one or two exceptions. Now, if I had only done as these anti-Lecompton men who voted for the English bill in Congress, pledging themselves to refuse to admit Kansas if she refused to become a slave State until she had a population of 93,420, and then returned to their people, forfeited their pledge, and made a new pledge to admit Kansas at any time she applied, without regard to population, I would have had no trouble. You saw the whole power and patronage of the Federal Government wielded in Indiana, Ohio, and Pennsylvania to re-elect anti-Lecompton men to Congress who voted against Lecompton, then voted for the English bill, and then denounced the English bill, and pledged themselves to their people to disregard it. My sin consists in not having given a pledge, and then in not having afterward forfeited it. For that reason, in this State, every postmaster, every route agent, every collector of the ports, and every Federal office-holder forfeits his head the moment he expresses a preference for the Democratic candidates against Lincoln and his Abolition associates. A Democratic Administration which we helped to bring into power deems it consistent with its fidelity to principle and its regard to duty to wield its power in this State in behalf of the Republican

Abolition candidates in every county and every Congressional District against the Democratic party. All I have to say in reference to the matter is, that if that Administration have not regard enough for principle, if they are not sufficiently attached to the creed of the Democratic party, to bury forever their personal hostilities in order to succeed in carrying out our glorious principles, I have. I have no personal difficulty with Mr. Buchanan or his Cabinet. He chose to make certain recommendations to Congress, as he had a right to do, on the Lecompton question. I could not vote in favor of them. I had as much right to judge for myself how I should vote as he had how he should recommend. He undertook to say to me, "If you do not vote as I tell you I will take off the heads of your friends." I replied to him, "You did not elect me. I represent Illinois, and I am accountable to Illinois, as my constituency, and to God; but not to the President or to any other power on earth."

And now this warfare is made on me because I would not surrender my convictions of duty, because I would not abandon my constituency, and receive the orders of the executive authorities how I should vote in the Senate of the United States. I hold that an attempt to control the Senate on the part of the Executive is subversive of the principles of our Constitution. The Executive department is independent of the Senate, and the Senate is independent of the President. In matters of legislation the President has a veto on the action of the Senate, and in appointments and treaties the Senate has a veto on the President.   He has no more right to tell me how I shall vote on his appointments than I have to tell him whether he shall veto or approve a bill that the Senate has passed. Whenever you recognize the right of the Executive to say to a senator, "Do this, or I will take off the heads of your friends," you convert this government from a republic into a despotism. Whenever you recognize the right of a President to say to a member of Congress, "Vote as I tell you, or I will bring a power to bear against you at home which will crush you," you destroy the independence of the representative, and convert him into a tool of Executive power. I resisted this invasion of the constitutional rights of a senator, and I intend to resist it as long as I have a voice to speak or a vote to give.   Yet Mr. Buchanan cannot provoke me to abandon one iota of Democratic principles out of revenge or hostility to his course. I stand by the platform of the Democratic party, and by its organization, and support its nominees. If there are any who choose to bolt, the fact only shows that they are not as good Democrats as I am.

My friends, there never was a time when it was as important for the Democratic party, for all national men, to rally and stand together, as it is to-day. We find all sectional men giving up past differences and continuing the one question of slavery; and when we find sectional men thus uniting, we should unite to resist them and their treasonable designs. Such was the case in 1850, when Clay left the quiet and peace of his home, and again entered upon public life to quell agitation and restore peace to a distracted Union. Then we Democrats, with Cass at our head, welcomed Henry Clay, whom the whole nation regarded as having been preserved by God for the times. He became our leader in that great fight, and we rallied around him the same as the Whigs rallied around old Hickory in 1832 to put down nullification. Thus you see that whilst Whigs and Democrats fought fearlessly in old times about banks, the tariff, distribution, the specie circular, and the sub-treasury, all united as a band of brothers when the peace, harmony, or integrity of the Union was imperiled. It was so in 1850, when Abolitionism had even so far divided this country, North and South, as to endanger the peace of the Union; Whigs and Democrats united in establishing the Compromise measures of that year and restoring tranquillity and good feeling. These measures passed on the joint action of the two parties. They rested on the great principle that the people of each State and each Territory should be left perfectly free to form and regulate their domestic institutions to suit themselves. You Whigs and we Democrats justified them in that principle. In 1854, when it became necessary to organize the Territories of Kansas and Nebraska, I brought forward the bill on the same principle. In the Kansas-Nebraska Bill you find it declared to be the true intent and meaning of the act not to legislate slavery into any State or Territory, nor to exclude it therefrom, but to leave the people thereof perfectly free to form and regulate their domestic institutions in their own

way. I stand on that same platform in 1858 that
I did in 1850, 1854, and 1856. The Washington
Union, pretending to be the organ of the Administration, in the number of the 5th of this month devotes
three columns and a half to establish these propositions: first, that Douglas, in his Freeport speech,
held the same doctrine that he did in his Nebraska
Bill in 1854; second, that in 1854 Douglas justified
the Nebraska Bill upon the ground that it was based
upon the same principle as Clay's Compromise
measures of 1850. The *Union* thus proved that
Douglas was the same in 1858 that he was in 1856,
1854, and 1850, and consequently argued that he was
never a Democrat. Is it not funny that I was never
a Democrat? There is no pretence that I have
changed a hair's breadth. The *Union* proves by
my speeches that I explained the Compromise
measures of 1850 just as I do now, and that I explained the Kansas and Nebraska Bill in 1854 just
as I did in my Freeport speech, and yet says that I
am not a Democrat, and cannot be trusted, because I
have not changed during the whole of that time. It
has occurred to me that in 1854 the author of the
Kansas and Nebraska Bill was considered a pretty
good Democrat. It has occurred to me that in 1856,
when I was exerting every nerve and every energy
for James Buchanan, standing on the same platform
then that I do now, that I was a pretty good Democrat. They now tell me that I am not a Democrat,
because I assert that the people of a Territory, as
well as those of a State, have the right to decide for
themselves whether slavery can or cannot exist in

such Territory. Let me read what James Buchanan said on that point when he accepted the Democratic nomination for the presidency in 1856. In his letter of acceptance, he used the following language:

"The recent legislation of Congress respecting domestic slavery, derived as it has been from the original and pure fountain of legitimate political power, the will of the majority, promises ere long to allay the dangerous excitement. This legislation is founded upon principles as ancient as free government itself, and, in accordance with them, has simply declared that the people of a Territory, like those of a State, shall decide for themselves whether slavery shall or shall not exist within their limits."

Dr. Hope will there find my answer to the question he propounded to me before I commenced speaking. Of course, no man will consider it an answer who is outside of the Democratic organization, bolts Democratic nominations, and indirectly aids to put Abolitionists into power over Democrats. But whether Dr. Hope considers it an answer or not, every fairminded man will see that James Buchanan has answered the question, and has asserted that the people of a Territory, like those of a State, shall decide for themselves whether slavery shall or shall not exist within their limits. I answer specifically if you want a further answer, and say that while, under the decision of the Supreme Court, as recorded in the opinion of Chief Justice Taney, slaves are property like all other property, and can be carried into any Territory of the United States the same as any other description of property, yet when you get them there they are subject to the local law of the Territory just like all other property. You will find in a recent speech delivered by that able and eloquent statesman Hon. Jefferson Davis, at Bangor, Maine, that he took the same view of this subject that I did in my Freeport speech. He there said:

"If the inhabitants of any Territory should refuse to enact such laws and police regulations as would give security to their property or to his, it would be rendered more or less valueless in proportion to the difficulties of holding it without such protection. In the case of property in the labor of man, or what is usually called slave property, the insecurity would be so great that the owner could not ordinarily retain it. Therefore, though the right would remain, the remedy being withheld, it would follow that the owner would be practically debarred, by the circumstances of the case, from taking slave property into a Territory where the sense of the inhabitants was opposed to its introduction. So much for the oft-repeated fallacy of forcing slavery upon any community."

You will also find that the distinguished Speaker of the present House of Representatives, Hon. Jas. L. Orr, construed the Kansas and Nebraska Bill in this same way in 1856, and also that great intellect of the South, Alex. H. Stephens, put the same construction upon it in Congress that I did in my Freeport speech. The whole South are rallying to the support of the doctrine that if the people of a Territory want slavery, they have a right to have it, and

if they do not want it, that no power on earth can
force it upon them.   I hold that there is no principle
on earth more sacred to all the friends of freedom
than that which says that no institution, no law, no
constitution, should be forced on an unwilling people contrary to their wishes; and I assert that the
Kansas and Nebraska Bill contains that principle.
It is the great principle contained in that bill.   It is
the principle on which James Buchanan was made
President.   Without that principle, he never would
have been made President of the United States.   I
will never violate or abandon that doctrine, if I have
to stand alone.   I have resisted the blandishments
and threats of power on the one side, and seduction
on the other, and have stood immovably for that
principle, fighting for it when assailed by Northern
mobs, or threatened by Southern hostility.   I have
defended it against the North and the South, and I
will defend it against whoever assails it, and I will
follow it wherever its logical conclusions lead me.   I
say to you that there is but one hope, one safety for
this country, and that is to stand immovably by
that principle which declares the right of each State
and each Territory to decide these questions for
themselves.   This government was founded on that
principle, and must be administered in the same
sense in which it was founded.

But the Abolition party really think that under
the Declaration of Independence the negro is equal
to the white man, and that negro equality is an
inalienable right conferred by the Almighty, and
hence that all human laws in violation of it are null

and void. With such men it is no use for me to argue. I hold that the signers of the Declaration of Independence had no reference to negroes at all when they declared all men to be created equal. They did not mean negroes, nor the savage Indians, nor the Feejee Islanders, nor any other barbarous race. They were speaking of white men. They alluded to men of European birth and European descent,— to white men, and to none others,—when they declared that doctrine. I hold that this government was established on the white basis. It was established by white men for the benefit of white men and their posterity forever, and should be administered by white men, and none others. But it does not follow by any means, that merely because the negro is not a citizen, and merely because he is not our equal, that, therefore, he should be a slave. On the contrary, it does follow that we ought to extend to the negro race, and to all other dependent races, all the rights, all the privileges, and all the immunities which they can exercise consistently with the safety of society. Humanity requires that we should give them all these privileges; Christianity commands that we should extend those privileges to them. The question then arises, What are those privileges, and what is the nature and extent of them? My answer is, that that is a question which each State must answer for itself. We in Illinois have decided it for ourselves. We tried slavery, kept it up for twelve years, and, finding that it was not profitable, we abolished it for that reason, and became a free State. We adopted in its stead the policy that a negro in this State shall not be a slave and shall not be a citizen. We have a right to adopt that policy. For my part, I think it is a wise and sound policy for us. You in Missouri must judge for yourselves whether it is a wise policy for you. If you choose to follow our example, very good; if you reject it, still well,—it is your business, not ours. So with Kentucky. Let Kentucky adopt a policy to suit herself. If we do not like it we will keep away from it; and if she does not like ours, let her stay at home, mind her own business, and let us alone. If the people of all the States will act on that great principle, and each State mind its own business, attend to its own affairs, take care of its own negroes, and not meddle with its neighbors, then there will be peace between the North and the South, the East and the West, throughout the whole Union.

Why can we not thus have peace? Why should we thus allow a sectional party to agitate this country, to array the North against the South, and convert us into enemies instead of friends, merely that a few ambitious men may ride into power on a sectional hobby? How long is it since these ambitious Northern men wished for a sectional organization? Did any one of them dream of a sectional party as long as the North was the weaker section and the South the stronger? Then all were opposed to sectional parties; but the moment the North obtained the majority in the House and Senate by the admission of California, and could elect a President without the aid of Southern votes, that moment ambitious Northern men formed a scheme to excite the North against the South, and make the people be governed in their votes by geographical lines, thinking that the North, being the stronger section, would outvote the South, and consequently they, the leaders, would ride into office on a sectional hobby.   I am told that my hour is out.   It was very short.

MR. LINCOLN'S REPLY.

LADIES AND GENTLEMEN: I have been somewhat, in my own mind, complimented by a large portion of Judge Douglas's speech,—I mean that portion which he devotes to the controversy between himself and the present Administration.   This is the seventh time Judge Douglas and myself have met in these joint discussions, and he has been gradually improving in regard to his war with the Administration.   At Quincy, day before yesterday, he was a little more severe upon the Administration than I had heard him upon any occasion, and I took pains to compliment him for it.   I then told him to give it to them with all the power he had; and as some of them were present, I told them I would be very much obliged if they would *give it to him* in about the same way.   I take it he has now vastly improved upon the attack he made then upon the Administration.   I flatter myself he has really taken my advice on this subject.   All I can say now is to re-commend to him and to them what I then commended,—to prosecute the war against one another in the most vigorous manner.   I say to them again: "Go it, husband!—Go it, bear!"

There is one other thing I will mention before I leave this branch of the discussion,—although I do not consider it much of my business, anyway. I refer to that part of the Judge's remarks where he undertakes to involve Mr. Buchanan in an inconsistency. He reads something from Mr. Buchanan, from which he undertakes to involve him in an inconsistency; and he gets something of a cheer for having done so. I would only remind the Judge that while he is very valiantly fighting for the Nebraska Bill and the repeal of the Missouri Compromise, it has been but a little while since he was the *valiant advocate of* the Missouri Compromise. I want to know if Buchanan has not as much right to be inconsistent as Douglas has? Has Douglas the *exclusive right*, in this country, of being *on all sides of all questions?* Is nobody allowed that high privilege but himself? Is he to have an entire *monopoly* on that subject?

So far as Judge Douglas addressed his speech to me, or so far as it was about me, it is my business to pay some attention to it. I have heard the Judge state two or three times what he has stated to-day,— that in a speech which I made at Springfield, Illinois, I had in a very especial manner complained that the Supreme Court in the Dred Scott case had decided that a negro could never be a citizen of the United States. I have omitted by some accident heretofore to analyze this statement, and it is required of me to notice it now. In point of fact it is *untrue*. I never have complained *especially* of the Dred Scott decision because it held that a negro could not be a citizen, and the Judge is always wrong when he says I ever did so complain of it. I have the speech here, and I will thank him or any of his friends to show where I said that a negro should be a citizen, and complained especially of the Dred Scott decision because it declared he could not be one. I have done no such thing; and Judge Douglas, so persistently insisting that I have done so, has strongly impressed me with the belief of a predetermination on his part to misrepresent me. He could not get his foundation for insisting that I was in favor of this negro equality anywhere else as well as he could by assuming that untrue proposition. Let me tell this audience what is true in regard to that matter; and the means by which they may correct me if I do not tell them truly is by a recurrence to the speech itself. I spoke of the Dred Scott decision in my Springfield speech, and I was then endeavoring to prove that the Dred Scott decision was a portion of a system or scheme to make slavery national in this country. I pointed out what things had been decided by the court. I mentioned as a fact that they had decided that a negro could not be a citizen; that they had done so, as I supposed, to deprive the negro, under all circumstances, of the remotest possibility of ever becoming a citizen and claiming the rights of a citizen of the United States under a certain clause of the Constitution. I stated that, without making any complaint of it at all. I then went on and stated the other points decided in the case; namely, that the bringing of a negro into the State of Illinois and holding him in slavery for two years here was a

matter in regard to which they would not decide
whether it would make him free or not; that they
decided the further point that taking him into a
United States Territory where slavery was prohibited
by Act of Congress did not make him free, because
that Act of Congress, as they held, was unconstitutional. I mentioned these three things as making
up the points decided in that case. I mentioned
them in a lump, taken in connection with the introduction of the Nebraska Bill, and the amendment of
Chase, offered at the time, declaratory of the right
of the people of the Territories to *exclude slavery*,
which was voted down by the friends of the bill. I
mentioned all these things together, as evidence
tending to prove a combination and conspiracy to
make the institution of slavery national. In that
connection and in that way I mentioned the decision
on the point that a negro could not be a citizen, and
in no other connection.

Out of this Judge Douglas builds up his beautiful
fabrication of my purpose to introduce a perfect
social and political equality between the white and
black races. His assertion that I made an "especial
objection" (that is his exact language) to the decision on this account is untrue in point of fact.

Now, while I am upon this subject, and as Henry
Clay has been alluded to, I desire to place myself,
in connection with Mr. Clay, as nearly right before
this people as may be. I am quite aware what the
Judge's object is here by all these allusions. He
knows that we are before an audience having strong
sympathies southward, by relationship, place of

birth, and so on. He desires to place me in an extremely Abolition attitude. He read upon a former occasion, and alludes, without reading, to-day to a portion of a speech which I delivered in Chicago. In his quotations from that speech, as he has made them upon former occasions, the extracts were taken in such a way as, I suppose, brings them within the definition of what is called *garbling*,—taking portions of a speech which, when taken by themselves, do not present the entire sense of the speaker as expressed at the time. I propose, therefore, out of that same speech, to show how one portion of it which he skipped over (taking an extract before and an extract after) will give a different idea, and the true idea I intended to convey. It will take me some little time to read it, but I believe I will occupy the time that way.

You have heard him frequently allude to my controversy with him in regard to the Declaration of Independence. I confess that I have had a struggle with Judge Douglas on that matter, and I will try briefly to place myself right in regard to it on this occasion. I said—and it is between the extracts Judge Douglas has taken from this speech, and put in his published speeches:

"It may be argued that there are certain conditions that make necessities and impose them upon us, and to the extent that a necessity is imposed upon a man he must submit to it. I think that was the condition in which we found ourselves when we established this government. We had slaves among us, we could not get our Constitution unless we permitted them to remain

in slavery, we could not secure the good we did secure
if we grasped for more; and having by necessity submitted to that much, it does not destroy the principle
that is the charter of our liberties. Let the charter remain as our standard."

Now, I have upon all occasions declared as strongly
as Judge Douglas against the disposition to interfere
with the existing institution of slavery. You hear
me read it from the same speech from which he takes
garbled extracts for the purpose of proving upon me
a disposition to interfere with the institution of
slavery, and establish a perfect social and political
equality between negroes and white people.

Allow me while upon this subject briefly to present
one other extract from a speech of mine, more than a
year ago, at Springfield, in discussing this very same
question, soon after Judge Douglas took his ground
that negroes were not included in the Declaration of
Independence:

"I think the authors of that notable instrument intended to include *all* men, but they did not mean to declare all men equal *in all respects*. They did not mean
to say all men were equal in color, size, intellect, moral
development, or social capacity. They defined with
tolerable distinctness in what they did consider all men
created equal,—equal in certain inalienable rights, among
which are life, liberty, and the pursuit of happiness.
This they said, and this they meant. They did not mean
to assert the obvious untruth that all were then actually
enjoying that equality, or yet that they were about to
confer it immediately upon them. In fact they had no
power to confer such a boon. They meant simply to

declare the *right*, so that the *enforcement* of it might follow as fast as circumstances should permit.

"They meant to set up a standard maxim for free society which should be familiar to all,—constantly looked to, constantly labored for, and even, though never perfectly attained, constantly approximated, and thereby constantly spreading and deepening its influence, and augmenting the happiness and value of life to all people, of all colors, everywhere."

There again are the sentiments I have expressed in regard to the Declaration of Independence upon a former occasion,—sentiments which have been put in print and read wherever anybody cared to know what so humble an individual as myself chose to say in regard to it.

At Galesburgh, the other day, I said, in answer to Judge Douglas, that three years ago there never had been a man, so far as I knew or believed, in the whole world, who had said that the Declaration of Independence did not include negroes in the term "all men." I reassert it to-day. I assert that Judge Douglas and all his friends may search the whole records of the country, and it will be a matter of great astonishment to me if they shall be able to find that one human being three years ago had ever uttered the astounding sentiment that the term "all men" in the Declaration did not include the negro. Do not let me be misunderstood. I know that more than three years ago there were men who, finding this assertion constantly in the way of their schemes to bring about the ascendency and perpetuation of slavery, *denied the truth of it*. I know that Mr. Calhoun and all the politicians of his school denied the truth of the Declaration. I know that it ran along in the mouth of some Southern men for a period of years, ending at last in that shameful, though rather forcible, declaration of Pettit of Indiana, upon the floor of the United States Senate, that the Declaration of Independence was in that respect "a self-evident lie," rather than a self-evident truth. But I say, with a perfect knowledge of all this hawking at the Declaration without directly attacking it, that three years ago there never had lived a man who had ventured to assail it in the sneaking way of pretending to believe it, and then asserting it did not include the negro. I believe the first man who ever said it was Chief Justice Taney in the Dred Scott case, and the next to him was our friend Stephen A. Douglas. And now it has become the catchword of the entire party. I would like to call upon his friends everywhere to consider how they have come in so short a time to view this matter in a way so entirely different from their former belief; to ask whether they are not being borne along by an irresistible current,—whither, they know not.

In answer to my proposition at Galesburgh last week, I see that some man in Chicago has got up a letter, addressed to the Chicago *Times*, to show, as he professes, that somebody *had* said so before; and he signs himself "An Old-Line Whig," if I remember correctly. In the first place, I would say he *was not* an old-line Whig. I am somewhat acquainted with old-line Whigs from the origin to the end of that party; I became pretty well acquainted with them,

and I know they always had some sense, whatever
else you could ascribe to them.   I know there never
was one who had not more sense than to try to show
by the evidence he produces that some men had,
prior to the time I named, said that negroes were not
included in the term "all men" in the Declaration of
Independence.   What is the evidence he produces?
I will bring forward *his* evidence, and let you see
what *he* offers by way of showing that somebody
more than three years ago had said negroes were not
included in the Declaration.   He brings forward
part of a speech from Henry Clay,—*the* part of *the*
speech of Henry Clay which I used to bring forward
to prove precisely the contrary.   I guess we are surrounded to some extent to-day by the old friends of
Mr. Clay, and they will be glad to hear anything
from that authority.   While he was in Indiana a
man presented a petition to liberate his negroes, and
he (Mr. Clay) made a speech in answer to it, which I
suppose he carefully wrote out himself and caused
to be published.   I have before me an extract from
that speech which constitutes the evidence this pretended "Old-Line Whig" at Chicago brought forward to show that Mr. Clay did n't suppose the negro
was included in the Declaration of Independence.
Hear what Mr. Clay said:

"And what is the foundation of this appeal to me in
Indiana to liberate the slaves under my care in Kentucky?   It is a general declaration in the act announcing
to the world the independence of the thirteen American
colonies, that all men are created equal.   Now, as an
abstract principle, *there is no doubt of the truth of that*

declaration; and it is desirable, *in the original construction of society and in organized societies,* to keep it in view as a great fundamental principle. But, then, I apprehend that in no society that ever did exist, or ever shall be formed, was or can the equality asserted among the members of the human race be practically enforced and carried out. There are portions, large portions,—women, minors, insane, culprits, transient sojourners,—that will always probably remain subject to the government of another portion of the community.

"That declaration, whatever may be the extent of its import, was made by the delegations of the thirteen States. In most of them slavery existed, and had long existed, and was established by law. It was introduced and forced upon the colonies by the paramount law of England. Do you believe that in making that declaration the States that concurred in it intended that it should be tortured into a virtual emancipation of all the slaves within their respective limits? Would Virginia and other Southern States have ever united in a declaration which was to be interpreted into an abolition of slavery among them? Did any one of the thirteen colonies entertain such a design or expectation? To impute such a secret and unavowed purpose, would be to charge a political fraud upon the noblest band of patriots that ever assembled in council,—a fraud upon the Confederacy of the Revolution; a fraud upon the union of those States whose Constitution not only recognized the lawfulness of slavery, but permitted the importation of slaves from Africa until the year 1808."

This is the entire quotation brought forward to prove that somebody previous to three years ago had said the negro was not included in the term "all

men" in the Declaration.   How does it do so?   In
what way has it a tendency to prove that?   Mr. Clay
says *it is true as an abstract principle* that all men are
created equal, but that we cannot practically apply it
in all cases.   He illustrates this by bringing forward
the cases of females, minors, and insane persons,
with whom it cannot be enforced; but he says it is
true as an abstract principle in the organization of
society as well as in organized society and it should be
kept in view as a fundamental principle.   Let me
read a few words more before I add some comments
of my own.   Mr. Clay says, a little further on:

"I desire no concealment of my opinions in regard to
the institution of slavery.   I look upon it as a great evil,
and deeply lament that we have derived it from the
parental government and from our ancestors.   I wish
every slave in the United States was in the country of
his ancestors.   But here they are, and the question is,
How can they be best dealt with?   If a state of nature
existed, and we were about to lay the foundations of society, *no man would be more strongly opposed than I should
be to incorporate the institution of slavery among its elements.*"

Now, here in this same book, in this same speech,
in this same extract, brought forward to prove that
Mr. Clay held that the negro was not included in the
Declaration of Independence, is no such statement
on his part, but the declaration *that it is a great
fundamental truth* which should be constantly kept
in view in the organization of society and in societies
already organized.   But if I say a word about it; if

I attempt, as Mr. Clay said all good men ought to do, to keep it in view; if, in this "organized society," I ask to have the public eye turned upon it; if I ask, in relation to the organization of new Territories, that the public eye should be turned upon it,— forthwith I am vilified as you hear me to-day. What have I done that I have not the license of Henry Clay's illustrious example here in doing? Have I done aught that I have not his authority for, while maintaining that in organizing new Territories and societies this fundamental principle should be regarded, and in organized society holding it up to the public view and recognizing what *he* recognized as the great principle of free government?

And when this new principle—this new proposition that no human being ever thought of three years ago —is brought forward, *I combat it* as having an evil tendency, if not an evil design. I combat it as having a tendency to dehumanize the negro, to take away from him the right of ever striving to be a man. I combat it as being one of the thousand things constantly done in these days to prepare the public mind to make property, and nothing but property, of the *negro in all the States of this Union.*

But there is a point that I wish, before leaving this part of the discussion, to ask attention to. I have read and I repeat the words of Henry Clay:

"I desire no concealment of my opinions in regard to the institution of slavery. I look upon it as a great evil, and deeply lament that we have derived it from the parental government and from our ancestors. I wish every slave in the United States was in the country of

his ancestors. But here they are; the question is, How
can they best be dealt with? If a state of nature existed, and we were about to lay the foundations of
society, no man would be more strongly opposed than I
should be to incorporate the institution of slavery among
its elements."

The principle upon which I have insisted in this
canvass is in relation to laying the foundations of new
societies. I have never sought to apply these
principles to the old States for the purpose of abolish-
ing slavery in those States. It is nothing but a
miserable perversion of what I *have* said, to assume
that I have declared Missouri, or any other slave
State, shall emancipate her slaves; I have proposed
no such thing. But when Mr. Clay says that in
laying the foundations of society in our Territories
where it does not exist, he would be opposed to the
introduction of slavery as an element, I insist that
we have *his warrant*—his license—for insisting upon
the exclusion of that element which he declared in
such strong and emphatic language *was most hateful
to him.*

Judge Douglas has again referred to a Springfield
speech in which I said "a house divided against itself
cannot stand." The Judge has so often made the
entire quotation from that speech that I can make
it from memory. I used this language:

"We are now far into the fifth year since a policy was
initiated with the avowed object and confident promise
of putting an end to the slavery agitation. Under the
operation of this policy, that agitation has not only not

ceased, but has constantly augmented. In my opinion
it will not cease until a crisis shall have been reached and
passed. 'A house divided against itself cannot stand.'
I believe this government cannot endure permanently,
half slave and half free. I do not expect the house to
fall, but I do expect it will cease to be divided. It will
become all one thing, or all the other. Either the opponents of slavery will arrest the further spread of it,
and place it where the public mind shall rest in the belief
that it is in the course of ultimate extinction, or its
advocates will push it forward till it shall become alike
lawful in all the States,—old as well as new, North as well
as South."

That extract and the sentiments expressed in it
have been extremely offensive to Judge Douglas. He
has warred upon them as Satan wars upon the Bible.
His perversions upon it are endless. Here now are
my views upon it in brief:

I said we were now far into the fifth year since a
policy was initiated with the avowed object and
confident promise of putting an end to the slavery
agitation. Is it not so? When that Nebraska Bill
was brought forward four years ago last January,
was it not for the "avowed object" of putting an
end to the slavery agitation? We were to have no
more agitation in Congress; it was all to be banished
to the Territories. By the way, I will remark here
that, as Judge Douglas is very fond of compliment-
ing Mr. Crittenden in these days, Mr. Crittenden has
said there was a falsehood in that whole business,
for there was *no slavery agitation at that time to allay.*
We were for a little while *quiet* on the troublesome

thing, and that very allaying plaster of Judge Douglas's stirred it up again. But was it not understood or intimated with the "confident promise" of putting an end to the slavery agitation? Surely it was. In every speech you heard Judge Douglas make, until he got into this "imbroglio," as they call it, with the Administration about the Lecompton Constitution, every speech on that Nebraska Bill was full of his felicitations that we were *just at the end* of the slavery agitation. The last tip of the last joint of the old serpent's tail was just drawing out of view. But has it proved so? I have asserted that under that policy that agitation "has not only not ceased, but has constantly augmented." When was there ever a greater agitation in Congress than last winter? When was it as great in the country as to-day?

There was a collateral object in the introduction of that Nebraska policy, which was to clothe the people of the Territories with a superior degree of self-government, beyond what they had ever had before. The first object and the main one of conferring upon the people a higher degree of "self-government" is a question of fact to be determined by you in answer to a single question. Have you ever heard or known of a people anywhere on earth who had as little to do as, in the first instance of its use, the people of Kansas had with this same right of "self-government"? In its main policy and in its collateral object, *it has been nothing but a living, creeping lie from the time of its introduction till to-day.*

I have intimated that I thought the agitation

would not cease until a crisis should have been reached and passed. I have stated in what way I thought it would be reached and passed. I have said that it might go one way or the other. We might, by arresting the further spread of it, and placing it where the fathers originally placed it, put it where the public mind should rest in the belief that it was in the course of ultimate extinction. Thus the agitation may cease. It may be pushed forward until it shall become alike lawful in all the States, old as well as new, North as well as South. I have said, and I repeat, my wish is that the further spread of it may be arrested, and that it may be placed where the public mind shall rest in the belief that it is in the course of ultimate extinction. I have expressed that as my wish. I entertain the opinion, upon evidence sufficient to my mind, that the fathers of this government placed that institution where the public mind *did* rest in the belief that it was in the course of ultimate extinction. Let me ask why they made provision that the source of slavery—the African slave-trade—should be cut off at the end of twenty years? Why did they make provision that in all the new territory we owned at that time slavery should be forever inhibited? Why stop its spread in one direction, and cut off its source in another, if they did not look to its being placed in the course of its ultimate extinction?

Again: the institution of slavery is only mentioned in the Constitution of the United States two or three times, and in neither of these cases does the word "slavery" or "negro race" occur; but covert language is used each time, and for a purpose full of significance. What is the language in regard to the prohibition of the African slave-trade? It runs in about this way: "The migration or importation of such persons as any of the States now existing shall think proper to admit, shall not be prohibited by the Congress prior to the year one thousand eight hundred and eight."

The next allusion in the Constitution to the question of slavery and the black race is on the subject of the basis of representation, and there the language used is:

"Representatives and direct taxes shall be apportioned among the several States which may be included within this Union, according to their respective numbers, which shall be determined by adding to the whole number of free persons, including those bound to service for a term of years, and excluding Indians not taxed,—three-fifths of all other persons."

It says "persons," not slaves, not negroes; but this "three-fifths" can be applied to no other class among us than the negroes.

Lastly, in the provision for the reclamation of fugitive slaves, it is said: "No person held to service or labor in one State, under the laws thereof, escaping into another, shall in consequence of any law or regulation therein be discharged from such service or labor, but shall be delivered up, on claim of the party to whom such service or labor may be due." There again there is no mention of the word "negro" or of slavery. In all three of these places, being the only allusions to slavery in the instrument, covert language is used. Language is used not suggesting that slavery existed or that the black race were among us. And I understand the contemporaneous history of those times to be that covert language was used with a purpose, and that purpose was that in our Constitution, which it was hoped and is still hoped will endure forever,—when it should be read by intelligent and patriotic men, after the institution of slavery had passed from among us,—there should be nothing on the face of the great charter of liberty suggesting that such a thing as negro slavery had ever existed among us. This is part of the evidence that the fathers of the government expected and intended the institution of slavery to come to an end. They expected and intended that it should be in the course of ultimate extinction. And when I say that I desire to see the further spread of it arrested, I only say I desire to see that done which the fathers have first done. When I say I desire to see it placed where the public mind will rest in the belief that it is in the course of ultimate extinction, I only say I desire to see it placed where they placed it. It is not true that our fathers, as Judge Douglas assumes, made this government part slave and part free. Understand the sense in which he puts it. He assumes that slavery is a rightful thing within itself, —was introduced by the framers of the Constitution. The exact truth is, that they found the institution existing among us, and they left it as they found it. But in making the government they left this institution with many clear marks of disapprobation upon it. They found slavery among them, and they left it among them because of the difficulty—the absolute impossibility—of its immediate removal. And when Judge Douglas asks me why we cannot let it remain part slave and part free, as the fathers of the government made it, he asks a question based upon an assumption which is itself a falsehood; and I turn upon him and ask him the question, when the policy that the fathers of the government had adopted in relation to this element among us was the best policy in the world, the only wise policy, the only policy that we can ever safely continue upon that will ever give us peace, unless this dangerous element masters us all and becomes a national institution,—*I turn upon him and ask him why he could not leave it alone.* I turn and ask him why he was driven to the necessity of introducing a *new policy* in regard to it. He has himself said he introduced a new policy. He said so in his speech on the 22d of March of the present year, 1858. I ask him why he could not let it remain where our fathers placed it. I ask, too, of Judge Douglas and his friends why we shall not again place this institution upon the basis on which the fathers left it. I ask you, when he infers that I am in favor of setting the free and slave States at war, when the institution was placed in that attitude by those who made the Constitution, *did they make any war?* If we had no war out of it when thus placed, wherein is the ground of belief that we shall have war out of it if we return to that policy? Have we had any peace upon this matter springing from any other basis? I maintain that we

have not. I have proposed nothing more than a
return to the policy of the fathers.

I confess, when I propose a certain measure of
policy, it is not enough for me that I do not intend
anything evil in the result, but it is incumbent on me
to show that it has not a *tendency* to that result. I
have met Judge Douglas in that point of view. I
have not only made the declaration that I do not
mean to produce a conflict between the States, but
I have tried to show by fair reasoning, and I think
I have shown to the minds of fair men, that I propose nothing but what has a most peaceful tendency.
The quotation that I happened to make in that
Springfield speech, that "a house divided against
itself cannot stand," and which has proved so offensive to the Judge, was part and parcel of the same
thing. He tries to show that variety in the domestic
institutions of the different States is necessary and
indispensable. I do not dispute it. I have no controversy with Judge Douglas about that. I shall
very readily agree with him that it would be foolish
for us to insist upon having a cranberry law here in
Illinois, where we have no cranberries, because they
have a cranberry law in Indiana, where they have
cranberries. I should insist that it would be exceedingly wrong in us to deny to Virginia the right
to enact oyster laws, where they have oysters,
because we want no such laws here. I understand,
I hope, quite as well as Judge Douglas or anybody
else, that the variety in the soil and climate and
face of the country, and consequent variety in the
industrial pursuits and productions of a country,

17

require systems of law conforming to this variety in the natural features of the country. I understand quite as well as Judge Douglas that if we here raise a barrel of flour more than we want, and the Louisianians raise a barrel of sugar more than they want, it is of mutual advantage to exchange. That produces commerce, brings us together, and makes us better friends. We like one another the more for it. And I understand as well as Judge Douglas, or anybody else, that these mutual accommodations are the cements which bind together the different parts of this Union; that instead of being a thing to "divide the house,"—figuratively expressing the Union,—they tend to sustain it; they are the props of the house, tending always to hold it up.

But when I have admitted all this, I ask if there is any parallel between these things and this institution of slavery? I do not see that there is any parallel at all between them. Consider it. When have we had any difficulty or quarrel amongst ourselves about the cranberry laws of Indiana, or the oyster laws of Virginia, or the pine-lumber laws of Maine, or the fact that Louisiana produces sugar, and Illinois flour? When have we had any quarrels over these things? When have we had perfect peace in regard to this thing which I say is an element of discord in this Union? We have sometimes had peace, but when was it? It was when the institution of slavery remained quiet where it was. We have had difficulty and turmoil whenever it has made a struggle to spread itself where it was not. I ask, then, if experience does not speak in thunder-tones, telling us that the policy which has given peace to the country heretofore, being returned to, gives the greatest promise of peace again. You may say, and Judge Douglas has intimated the same thing, that all this difficulty in regard to the institution of slavery is the mere agitation of office-seekers and ambitious Northern politicians. He thinks we want to get "his place," I suppose. I agree that there are office-seekers amongst us. The Bible says somewhere that we are desperately selfish. I think we would have discovered that fact without the Bible. I do not claim that I am any less so than the average of men, but I do claim that I am not more selfish than Judge Douglas.

But is it true that all the difficulty and agitation we have in regard to this institution of slavery spring from office-seeking, from the mere ambition of politicians? Is that the truth? How many times have we had danger from this question? Go back to the day of the Missouri Compromise. Go back to the Nullification question, at the bottom of which lay this same slavery question. Go back to the time of the annexation of Texas. Go back to the troubles that led to the Compromise of 1850. You will find that every time, with the single exception of the Nullification question, they sprung from an endeavor to spread this institution. There never was a party in the history of this country, and there probably never will be, of sufficient strength to disturb the general peace of the country. Parties themselves may be divided and quarrel on minor questions, yet it extends not beyond the parties themselves. But

does *not* this question make a disturbance outside of
political circles?   Does it not enter into the churches
and rend them asunder?   What divided the great
Methodist Church into two parts, North and South?
What has raised this constant disturbance in every
Presbyterian General Assembly that meets?   What
disturbed the Unitarian Church in this very city two
years ago?   What has jarred and shaken the great
American Tract Society recently, not yet splitting it,
but sure to divide it in the end?   Is it not this same
mighty, deep-seated power that somehow operates
on the minds of men, exciting and stirring them up
in every avenue of society,—in politics, in religion,
in literature, in morals, in all the manifold relations
of life?   Is this the work of politicians?   Is that
irresistible power, which for fifty years has shaken
the government and agitated the people, to be stilled
and subdued by pretending that it is an exceedingly
simple thing, and we ought not to talk about it?   If
you will get everybody else to stop talking about it,
I assure you I will quit before they have half done so.
But where is the philosophy or statesmanship which
assumes that you can quiet that disturbing element
in our society which has disturbed us for more than
half a century, which has been the only serious
danger that has threatened our institutions,—I say,
where is the philosophy or the statesmanship based
on the assumption that we are to quit talking about
it, and that the public mind is all at once to cease
being agitated by it?   Yet this is the policy here in
the North that Douglas is advocating,—that we are
to care nothing about it!   I ask you if it is not a

false philosophy. Is it not a false statesmanship that undertakes to build up a system of policy upon the basis of caring nothing about *the very thing that everybody does care the most about*—a thing which all experience has shown we care a very great deal about?

The Judge alludes very often in the course of his remarks to the exclusive right which the States have to decide the whole thing for themselves. I agree with him very readily that the different States have that right. He is but fighting a man of straw when he assumes that I am contending against the right of the States to do as they please about it. Our controversy with him is in regard to the new Territories. We agree that when the States come in as States they have the right and the power to do as they please. We have no power as citizens of the free States, or in our Federal capacity as members of the Federal Union through the General Government, to disturb slavery in the States where it exists. We profess constantly that we have no more inclination than belief in the power of the government to disturb it; yet we are driven constantly to defend ourselves from the assumption that we are warring upon the rights of the *States*. What I insist upon is, that the new Territories shall be kept free from it while in the Territorial condition. Judge Douglas assumes that we have no interest in them,—that we have no right whatever to interfere. I think we have some interest. I think that as white men we have. Do we not wish for an outlet for our surplus population, if I may so express myself? Do we not feel an interest in getting to that outlet with such institutions as we would like to have prevail there? If *you* go to the Territory opposed to slavery, and another man comes upon the same ground with his slave, upon the assumption that the things are equal, it turns out that he has the equal right all his way, and you have no part of it your way. If he goes in and makes it a slave Territory, and by consequence a slave State, is it not time that those who desire to have it a free State were on equal ground? Let me suggest it in a different way. How many Democrats are there about here ["A thousand"] who have left slave States and come into the free State of Illinois to get rid of the institution of slavery? [Another voice: 'A thousand and one."] I reckon there are a thousand and one. I will ask you, if the policy you are now advocating had prevailed when this country was in a Territorial condition, where would you have gone to get rid of it? Where would you have found your free State or Territory to go to? And when hereafter, for any cause, the people in this place shall desire to find new homes, if they wish to be rid of the institution, where will they find the place to go to?

Now, irrespective of the moral aspect of this question as to whether there is a right or wrong in enslaving a negro, I am still in favor of our new Territories being in such a condition that white men may find a home,—may find some spot where they can better their condition; where they can settle upon new soil and better their condition in life. I am in favor of this, not merely (I must say it here as I have elsewhere) for our own people who are born amongst us, but as an outlet for *free white people everywhere—*

the world over—in which Hans, and Baptiste, and
Patrick, and all other men from all the world, may
find new homes and better their conditions in life.

I have stated upon former occasions, and I may
as well state again, what I understand to be the real
issue in this controversy between Judge Douglas and
myself. On the point of my wanting to make war
between the free and the slave States, there has
been no issue between us. So, too, when he assumes
that I am in favor of introducing a perfect social and
political equality between the white and black races.
These are false issues, upon which Judge Douglas has
tried to force the controversy. There is no foundation in truth for the charge that I maintain either of
these propositions. The real issue in this controversy—the one pressing upon every mind—is the
sentiment on the part of one class that looks upon the
institution of slavery *as a wrong*, and of another class
that *does not* look upon it as a wrong. The sentiment
that contemplates the institution of slavery in this
country as a wrong is the sentiment of the Republican party. It is the sentiment around which all
their actions, all their arguments, circle, from which
all their propositions radiate. They look upon it as
being a moral, social, and political wrong; and while
they contemplate it as such, they nevertheless have
due regard for its actual existence among us, and the
difficulties of getting rid of it in any satisfactory way,
and to all the constitutional obligations thrown about
it. Yet, having a due regard for these, they desire a
policy in regard to it that looks to its not creating
any more danger. They insist that it should, as far

as may be, *be treated* as a wrong; and one of the methods of treating it as a wrong is to *make provision that it shall grow no larger*.   They also desire a policy that looks to a peaceful end of slavery at some time, as being wrong.   These are the views they entertain in regard to it as I understand them; and all their sentiments, all their arguments and propositions, are brought within this range.   I have said, and I repeat it here, that if there be a man amongst us who does not think that the institution of slavery is wrong in any one of the aspects of which I have spoken, he is misplaced, and ought not to be with us.   And if there be a man amongst us who is so impatient of it as a wrong as to disregard its actual presence among us and the difficulty of getting rid of it suddenly in a satisfactory way, and to disregard the constitutional obligations thrown about it, that man is misplaced if he is on our platform.   We disclaim sympathy with him in practical action.   He is not placed properly with us.

On this subject of treating it as a wrong, and limiting its spread, let me say a word.   Has anything ever threatened the existence of this Union save and except this very institution of slavery?   What is it that we hold most dear amongst us?   Our own liberty and prosperity.   What has ever threatened our liberty and prosperity, save and except this institution of slavery?   If this is true, how do you propose to improve the condition of things by enlarging slavery,—by spreading it out and making it bigger?   You may have a wen or cancer upon your person, and not be able to cut it out, lest you bleed to death;

but surely it is no way to cure it, to engraft it and
spread it over your whole body. That is no proper
way of treating what you regard a wrong. You see
this peaceful way of dealing with it as a wrong,—
restricting the spread of it, and not allowing it to go
into new countries where it has not already existed.
That is the peaceful way, the old-fashioned way, the
way in which the fathers themselves set us the
example.

On the other hand, I have said there is a sentiment
which treats it as *not* being wrong. That is the
Democratic sentiment of this day. I do not mean to
say that every man who stands within that range
positively asserts that it is right. That class will
include all who positively assert that it is right, and
all who, like Judge Douglas, treat it as indifferent
and do not say it is either right or wrong. These two
classes of men fall within the general class of those
who do not look upon it as a wrong. And if there
be among you anybody who supposes that he, as a
Democrat, can consider himself "as much opposed
to slavery as anybody," I would like to reason with
him. You never treat it as a wrong. What other
thing that you consider as a wrong do you deal with
as you deal with that? Perhaps you *say* it is wrong,
*but your leader never does, and you quarrel with any-
body who says it is wrong.* Although you pretend to
say so yourself, you can find no fit place to deal with
it as a wrong. You must not say anything about it
in the free States, *because it is not here.* You must
not say anything about it in the slave States,
because it is there. You must not say anything about

it in the pulpit, because that is religion, and has nothing to do with it. You must not say anything about it in politics, *because that will disturb the security of "my place."* There is no place to talk about it as being a wrong, although you say yourself it is a wrong. But, finally, you will screw yourself up to the belief that if the people of the slave States should adopt a system of gradual emancipation on the slavery question, you would be in favor of it. You would be in favor of it. You say that is getting it in the right place, and you would be glad to see it succeed. But you are deceiving yourself. You all know that Frank Blair and Gratz Brown, down there in St. Louis, undertook to introduce that system in Missouri. They fought as valiantly as they could for the system of gradual emancipation which you pretend you would be glad to see succeed. Now, I will bring you to the test. After a hard fight they were beaten, and when the news came over here, you threw up your hats and *hurrahed for Democracy.* More than that, take all the argument made in favor of the system you have proposed, and it carefully excludes the idea that there is anything wrong in the institution of slavery. The arguments to sustain that policy carefully exclude it. Even here to-day you heard Judge Douglas quarrel with me because I uttered a wish that it might sometime come to an end. Although Henry Clay could say he wished every slave in the United States was in the country of his ancestors, I am denounced by those pretending to respect Henry Clay for uttering a wish that it might sometime, in some peaceful way, come to an end. The Democratic policy in regard to that institution will not tolerate the merest breath, the slightest hint, of the least degree of wrong about it. Try it by some of Judge Douglas's arguments. He says he "don't care whether it is voted up or voted down" in the Territories. I do not care myself, in dealing with that expression, whether it is intended to be expressive of his individual sentiments on the subject, or only of the national policy he desires to have established. It is alike valuable for my purpose. Any man can say that who does not see anything wrong in slavery; but no man can logically say it who does see a wrong in it, because no man can logically say he don't care whether a wrong is voted up or voted down. He may say he don't care whether an indifferent thing is voted up or down, but he must logically have a choice between a right thing and a wrong thing. He contends that whatever community wants slaves has a right to have them. So they have, if it is not a wrong. But if it is a wrong, he cannot say people have a right to do wrong. He says that upon the score of equality slaves should be allowed to go in a new Territory, like other property. This is strictly logical if there is no difference between it and other property. If it and other property are equal, this argument is entirely logical. But if you insist that one is wrong and the other right, there is no use to institute a comparison between right and wrong. You may turn over everything in the Democratic policy from beginning to end, whether in the shape it takes on the statute book, in the shape it takes in the Dred

Scott decision, in the shape it takes in conversation, or the shape it takes in short maxim-like arguments, —it everywhere carefully excludes the idea that there is anything wrong in it.

That is the real issue. That is the issue that will continue in this country when these poor tongues of Judge Douglas and myself shall be silent. It is the eternal struggle between these two principles—right and wrong—throughout the world. They are the two principles that have stood face to face from the beginning of time, and will ever continue to struggle. The one is the common right of humanity, and the other the divine right of kings. It is the same principle in whatever shape it develops itself. It is the same spirit that says, "You work and toil and earn bread, and I 'll eat it." No matter in what shape it comes, whether from the mouth of a king who seeks to bestride the people of his own nation and live by the fruit of their labor, or from one race of men as an apology for enslaving another race, it is the same tyrannical principle. I was glad to express my gratitude at Quincy, and I re-express it here, to Judge Douglas,—*that he looks to no end of the institution of slavery.* That will help the people to see where the struggle really is. It will hereafter place with us all men who really do wish the wrong may have an end. And whenever we can get rid of the fog which obscures the real question, when we can get Judge Douglas and his friends to avow a policy looking to its perpetuation,—we can get out from among that class of men and bring them to the side of those who treat it as a wrong. Then there will soon be an end

of it, and that end will be its "ultimate extinction."
Whenever the issue can be distinctly made, and all
extraneous matter thrown out so that men can
fairly see the real difference between the parties, this
controversy will soon be settled, and it will be done
peaceably too. There will be no war, no violence.
It will be placed again where the wisest and best men
of the world placed it. Brooks of South Carolina
once declared that when this Constitution was
framed its framers did not look to the institution
existing until this day. When he said this, I think
he stated a fact that is fully borne out by the history
of the times. But he also said they were better and
wiser men than the men of these days, yet the men
of these days had experience which they had not,
and by the invention of the cotton-gin it became a
necessity in this country that slavery should be perpetual. I now say that, willingly or unwillingly,
purposely or without purpose, Judge Douglas has
been the most prominent instrument in changing
the position of the institution of slavery,—which the
fathers of the government expected to come to an
end ere this,—*and putting it upon Brooks's cotton-gin
basis;* placing it where he openly confesses he has no
desire there shall ever be an end of it.

I understand I have ten minutes yet. I will
employ it in saying something about this argument
Judge Douglas uses, while he sustains the Dred Scott
decision, that the people of the Territories can still
somehow exclude slavery. The first thing I ask
attention to is the fact that Judge Douglas constantly said, before the decision, that whether they

could or not, *was a question for the Supreme Court.*
But after the court had made the decision he virtu-
ally says it is *not* a question for the Supreme Court,
but for the people.   And how is it he tells us they
can exclude it?   He says it needs "police regulations," and that admits of "unfriendly legislation."
Although it is a right established by the Constitution
of the United States to take a slave into a Territory
of the United States and hold him as property, yet
unless the Territorial Legislature will give friendly
legislation, and more especially if they adopt unfriendly legislation, they can practically exclude
him.   Now, without meeting this proposition as a
matter of fact, I pass to consider the real constitutional obligation.   Let me take the gentleman who
looks me in the face before me, and let us suppose
that he is a member of the Territorial Legislature.
The first thing he will do will be to swear that he will
support the Constitution of the United States.   His
neighbor by his side in the Territory has slaves and
needs Territorial legislation to enable him to enjoy
that constitutional right.   Can he withhold the
legislation which his neighbor needs for the enjoyment of a right which is fixed in his favor in the Constitution of the United States which he has sworn to
support?   Can he withhold it without violating his
oath?   And, more especially, can he pass unfriendly
legislation to violate his oath?   Why, this is a
monstrous sort of talk about the Constitution of the
United States!   *There has never been as outlandish or
lawless a doctrine from the mouth of any respectable
man on earth.*   I do not believe it is a constitutional

right to hold slaves in a Territory of the United States. I believe the decision was improperly made and I go for reversing it. Judge Douglas is furious against those who go for reversing a decision. But he is for legislating it out of all force while the law itself stands. I repeat that there has never been so monstrous a doctrine uttered from the mouth of a respectable man.

I suppose most of us (I know it of myself) believe that the people of the Southern States are entitled to a Congressional Fugitive Slave law,—that is a right fixed in the Constitution. But it cannot be made available to them without Congressional legislation. In the Judge's language, it is a "barren right," which needs legislation before it can become efficient and valuable to the persons to whom it is guaranteed. And as the right is constitutional, I agree that the legislation shall be granted to it,—and that not that we like the institution of slavery. We profess to have no taste for running and catching niggers,—at least, I profess no taste for that job at all. Why then do I yield support to a Fugitive Slave law? Because I do not understand that the Constitution, which guarantees that right, can be supported without it. And if I believed that the right to hold a slave in a Territory was equally fixed in the Constitution with the right to reclaim fugitives, I should be bound to give it the legislation necessary to support it. I say that no man can deny his obligation to give the necessary legislation to support slavery in a Territory, who believes it is a constitutional right to have it there. No man can, who does not give the

Abolitionists an argument to deny the obligation enjoined by the Constitution to enact a Fugitive State law. Try it now. It is the strongest Abolition argument ever made. I say if that Dred Scott decision is correct, then the right to hold slaves in a Territory is equally a constitutional right with the right of a slaveholder to have his runaway returned. No one can show the distinction between them. The one is express, so that we cannot deny it. The other is construed to be in the Constitution, so that he who believes the decision to be correct believes in the right. And the man who argues that by unfriendly legislation, in spite of that constitutional right, slavery may be driven from the Territories, cannot avoid furnishing an argument by which Abolitionists may deny the obligation to return fugitives, and claim the power to pass laws unfriendly to the right of the slaveholder to reclaim his fugitive. I do not know how such an argument may strike a popular assembly like this, but I defy anybody to go before a body of men whose minds are educated to estimating evidence and reasoning, and show that there is an iota of difference between the constitutional right to reclaim a fugitive and the constitutional right to hold a slave, in a Territory, provided this Dred Scott decision is correct, I defy any man to make an argument that will justify unfriendly legislation to deprive a slaveholder of his right to hold his slave in a Territory, that will not equally, in all its length, breadth, and thickness, furnish an argument for nullifying the Fugitive Slave law. Why, there is not such an Abolitionist in the nation as Douglas, after all!

Mr. LINCOLN has concluded his remarks by saying that there is not such an Abolitionist as I am in all America. If he could make the Abolitionists of Illinois believe that, he would not have much show for the Senate. Let him make the Abolitionists believe the truth of that statement, and his political back is broken.

His first criticism upon me is the expression of his hope that the war of the Administration will be prosecuted against me and the Democratic party of this State with vigor. He wants that war prosecuted with vigor; I have no doubt of it. His hopes of success and the hopes of his party depend solely upon it. They have no chance of destroying the Democracy of this State except by the aid of Federal patronage. He has all the Federal office-holders here as his allies, running separate tickets against the Democracy to divide the party, although the leaders all intend to vote directly the Abolition ticket, and only leave the greenhorns to vote this separate ticket who refuse to go into the Abolition camp. There is something really refreshing in the thought that Mr. Lincoln is in favor of prosecuting one war vigorously. It is the first war that I ever knew him to be in favor of prosecuting. It is the first war that I ever knew him to believe to be just or constitutional. When the Mexican War was being waged, and the American army was surrounded by the enemy in Mexico, he thought that war was unconstitutional, unnecessary, and unjust. He thought it was not commenced on the right *spot*.

18

When I made an incidental allusion of that kind
in the joint discussion over at Charleston some weeks
ago, Lincoln, in replying, said that I, Douglas, had
charged him with voting against supplies for the
Mexican War, and then he reared up, full length, and
swore that he never voted against the supplies; that
it was a slander; and caught hold of Ficklin, who sat
on the stand, and said, "Here, Ficklin, tell the people
that it is a lie." Well, Ficklin, who had served in
Congress with him, stood up and told them all that
he recollected about it. It was that when George
Ashmun, of Massachusetts, brought forward a resolution declaring the war unconstitutional, unnecessary, and unjust, that Lincoln had voted for it.
"Yes," said Lincoln, "I did." Thus he confessed
that he voted that the war was wrong, that our
country was in the wrong, and consequently that the
Mexicans were in the right; but charged that I had
slandered him by saying that he voted against the
supplies. I never charged him with voting against
the supplies in my life, because I knew that he was
not in Congress when they were voted. The war was
commenced on the 13th day of May, 1846, and on
that day we appropriated in Congress ten millions
of dollars and fifty thousand men to prosecute it.
During the same session we voted more men and
more money, and at the next session we voted more
men and more money, so that by the time Mr. Lincoln
entered Congress we had enough men and enough
money to carry on the war, and had no occasion to
vote for any more. When he got into the House,
being opposed to the war, and not being able to stop

the supplies, because they had all gone forward, all he could do was to follow the lead of Corwin, and prove that the war was not begun on the right spot, and that it was unconstitutional, unnecessary, and wrong. Remember, too, that this he did after the war had been begun. It is one thing to be opposed to the declaration of a war, another and very different thing to take sides with the enemy against your own country after the war has been commenced. Our army was in Mexico at the time, many battles had been fought; our citizens, who were defending the honor of their country's flag, were surrounded by the daggers, the guns, and the poison of the enemy. Then it was that Corwin made his speech in which he declared that the American soldiers ought to be welcomed by the Mexicans with bloody hands and hospitable graves; then it was that Ashmun and Lincoln voted in the House of Representatives that the war was unconstitutional and unjust; and Ashmun's resolution, Corwin's speech, and Lincoln's vote were sent to Mexico and read at the head of the Mexican army, to prove to them that there was a Mexican party in the Congress of the United States who were doing all in their power to aid them. That a man who takes sides with the common enemy against his own country in time of war should rejoice in a war being made on me now, is very natural. And, in my opinion, no other kind of a man would rejoice in it.

Mr. Lincoln has told you a great deal to-day about his being an old-line Clay Whig. Bear in mind that there are a great many old Clay Whigs down in this

region. It is more agreeable, therefore, for him to
talk about the old Clay Whig party than it is for him
to talk Abolitionism. We did not hear much about
the old Clay Whig party up in the Abolition districts. How much of an old-line Henry Clay Whig
was he? Have you read General Singleton's speech
at Jacksonville? You know that General Singleton
was for twenty-five years the confidential friend of
Henry Clay in Illinois, and he testified that in 1847,
when the Constitutional Convention of this State
was in session, the Whig members were invited to a
Whig caucus at the house of Mr. Lincoln's brother-in-
law, where Mr. Lincoln proposed to throw Henry
Clay overboard and take up General Taylor in his
place, giving as his reason that if the Whigs did
not take up General Taylor the Democrats would.
Singleton testifies that Lincoln in that speech urged
as another reason for throwing Henry Clay overboard
that the Whigs had fought long enough for principle
and ought to begin to fight for success. Singleton
also testifies that Lincoln's speech did have the effect
of cutting Clay's throat, and that he (Singleton) and
others withdrew from the caucus in indignation.
He further states that when they got to Philadelphia
to attend the National Convention of the Whig party,
that Lincoln was there, the bitter and deadly enemy
of Clay, and that he tried to keep him (Singleton)
out of the Convention because he insisted on voting
for Clay, and Lincoln was determined to have Taylor.
Singleton says that Lincoln rejoiced with very great
joy when he found the mangled remains of the
murdered Whig statesman lying cold before him.

Now, Mr. Lincoln tells you that he is an old-line Clay Whig! General Singleton testifies to the facts I have narrated, in a public speech which has been printed and circulated broadcast over the State for weeks, yet not a lisp have we heard from Mr. Lincoln on the subject, except that he is an old Clay Whig.

What part of Henry Clay's policy did Lincoln ever advocate? He was in Congress in 1848-9, when the Wilmot Proviso warfare disturbed the peace and harmony of the country, until it shook the foundation of the Republic from its centre to its circumference. It was that agitation that brought Clay forth from his retirement at Ashland again to occupy his seat in the Senate of the United States, to see if he could not, by his great wisdom and experience, and the renown of his name, do something to restore peace and quiet to a disturbed country. Who got up that sectional strife that Clay had to be called upon to quell? I have heard Lincoln boast that he voted forty-two times for the Wilmot Proviso, and that he would have voted as many times more if he could. Lincoln is the man, in connection with Seward, Chase, Giddings, and other Abolitionists, who got up that strife that I helped Clay to put down. Henry Clay came back to the Senate in 1849, and saw that he must do something to restore peace to the country. The Union Whigs and the Union Democrats welcomed him, the moment he arrived, as the man for the occasion. We believed that he, of all men on earth, had been preserved by Divine Providence to guide us out of our difficulties, and we Democrats rallied under Clay then, as you Whigs in

Nullification time rallied under the banner of old Jackson, forgetting party when the country was in danger, in order that we might have a country first, and parties afterwards.

And this reminds me that Mr. Lincoln told you that the slavery question was the only thing that ever disturbed the peace and harmony of the Union. Did not Nullification once raise its head and disturb the peace of this Union in 1832? Was that the slavery question, Mr. Lincoln? Did not disunion raise its monster head during the last war with Great Britain? Was that the slavery question, Mr. Lincoln? The peace of this country has been disturbed three times, once during the war with Great Britain, once on the tariff question, and once on the slavery question. His argument, therefore, that slavery is the only question that has ever created dissension in the Union falls to the ground. It is true that agitators are enabled now to use this slavery question for the purpose of sectional strife. He admits that in regard to all things else, the principle that I advocate, making each State and Territory free to decide for itself, ought to prevail. He instances the cranberry laws and the oyster laws, and he might have gone through the whole list with the same effect. I say that all these laws are local and domestic, and that local and domestic concerns should be left to each State and each Territory to manage for itself. If agitators would acquiesce in that principle, there never would be any danger to the peace and harmony of the Union.

Mr. Lincoln tries to avoid the main issue by attacking the truth of my proposition that our fathers made this government divided into free and slave States, recognizing the right of each to decide all its local questions for itself. Did they not thus make it? It is true that they did not establish slavery in any of the States, or abolish it in any of them; but finding thirteen States, twelve of which were slave and one free, they agreed to form a government uniting them together as they stood, divided into free and slave States, and to guarantee forever to each State the right to do as it pleased on the slavery question. Having thus made the government, and conferred this right upon each State forever, I assert that this government can exist as they made it, divided into free and slave States, if any one State chooses to retain slavery. He says that he looks forward to a time when slavery shall be abolished everywhere. I look forward to a time when each State shall be allowed to do as it pleases. If it chooses to keep slavery forever, it is not my business, but its own; if it chooses to abolish slavery, it is its own business, —not mine. I care more for the great principle of self-government, the right of the people to rule, than I do for all the negroes in Christendom. I would not endanger the perpetuity of this Union, I would not blot out the great inalienable rights of the white man, for all the negroes that ever existed. Hence, I say, let us maintain this government on the principles that our fathers made it, recognizing the right of each State to keep slavery as long as its people determine, or to abolish it when they please. But Mr. Lincoln says that when our fathers made this government they did not look forward to the state of things now existing, and therefore he thinks the doctrine was wrong; and he quotes Brooks of South Carolina to prove that our fathers then thought that probably slavery would be abolished by each State acting for itself before this time. Suppose they did; suppose they did not foresee what has occurred,—does that change the principles of our government? They did not, probably, foresee the telegraph that transmits intelligence by lightning, nor did they foresee the railroads that now form the bonds of union between the different States, or the thousand mechanical inventions that have elevated mankind. But do these things change the principles of the government? Our fathers, I say, made this government on the principle of the right of each State to do as it pleases in its own domestic affairs, subject to the Constitution, and allowed the people of each to apply to every new change of circumstances such remedy as they may see fit to improve their condition. This right they have for all time to come.

Mr. Lincoln went on to tell you that he does not at all desire to interfere with slavery in the States where it exists, nor does his party. I expected him to say that down here. Let me ask him, then, how he expects to put slavery in the course of ultimate extinction everywhere, if he does not intend to interfere with it in the States where it exists? He says that he will prohibit it in all Territories, and the inference is, then, that unless they make free States out of them he will keep them out of the Union; for, mark you, he did not say whether or not he would vote to admit Kansas with slavery or not, as her people might apply (he forgot that, as usual, etc.) : he did not say whether or not he was in favor of bringing the Territories now in existence into the Union on the principle of Clay's Compromise measures on the slavery question. I told you that he would not. His idea is that he will prohibit slavery in all the Territories and thus force them all to become free States, surrounding the slave States with a cordon of free States, and hemming them in, keeping the slaves confined to their present limits whilst they go on multiplying, until the soil on which they live will no longer feed them, and he will thus be able to put slavery in a course of ultimate extinction by starvation. He will extinguish slavery in the Southern States as the French general exterminated the Algerines when he smoked them out. He is going to extinguish slavery by surrounding the Slave States, hemming in the slaves, and starving them out of existence, as you smoke a fox out of his hole. He intends to do that in the name of humanity and Christianity, in order that we may get rid of the terrible crime and sin entailed upon our fathers of holding slaves. Mr. Lincoln makes out that line of policy, and appeals to the moral sense of justice and to the Christian feeling of the community to sustain him. He says that any man who holds to the contrary doctrine is in the position of the king who claimed to govern by divine right. Let us examine for a moment and see what principle it was that overthrew the divine right of George the Third to govern us. Did not these colonies rebel because the British Parliament had no right to pass laws concerning our property and domestic and private institutions without our consent? We demanded that the British Government should not pass such laws unless they gave us representation in the body passing them; and this the British Government insisting on doing, we went to war, on the principle that the home government should not control and govern distant colonies without giving them a representation. Now, Mr. Lincoln proposes to govern the Territories without giving them a representation, and calls on Congress to pass laws controlling their property and domestic concerns without their consent and against their will. Thus, he asserts for his party the indentical principle asserted by George III. and the Tories of the Revolution.

I ask you to look into these things, and then tell me whether the Democracy or the Abolitionists are right. I hold that the people of a Territory, like those of a State (I use the language of Mr. Buchanan in his Letter of Acceptance), have the right to decide for themselves whether slavery shall or shall not exist within their limits. The point upon which Chief Justice Taney expresses his opinion is simply this, that slaves, being property, stand on an equal footing with other property, and consequently that the owner has the same right to carry that property into a Territory that he has any other, subject to the same conditions. Suppose that one of your merchants was to take fifty or one hundred thousand dollars' worth of liquors to Kansas. He has a right to go there, under that decision; but when he gets there he finds the Maine liquor law in force, and what can he do with his property after he gets it there? He cannot sell it, he cannot use it; it is subject to the local law, and that law is against him, and the best thing he can do with it is to bring it back into Missouri or Illinois and sell it. If you take negroes to Kansas, as Colonel Jefferson Davis said in his Bangor speech, from which I have quoted to-day, you must take them there subject to the local law. If the people want the institution of slavery, they will protect and encourage it; but if they do not want it, they will withhold that protection, and the absence of local legislation protecting slavery excludes it as completely as a positive prohibition. You slaveholders of Missouri might as well understand, what you know practically, that you cannot carry slavery where the people do not want it. All you have a right to ask is that the people shall do as they please: if they want slavery, let them have it; if they do not want it, allow them to refuse to encourage it.

My friends, if, as I have said before, we will only live up to this great fundamental principle, there will be peace between the North and the South. Mr. Lincoln admits that, under the Constitution, on all domestic questions, except slavery, we ought not to interfere with the people of each State. What right have we to interfere with slavery any more than we have to interfere with any other question? He says that this slavery question is now the bone of contention. Why? Simply because agitators have combined in all the free States to make war upon it.

Suppose the agitators in the States should combine in one half of the Union to make war upon the railroad system of the other half? They would thus be driven to the same sectional strife. Suppose one section makes war upon any other peculiar institution of the opposite section, and the same strife is produced. The only remedy and safety is that we shall stand by the Constitution as our fathers made it, obey the laws as they are passed, while they stand the proper test, and sustain the decisions of the Supreme Court and the constituted authorities.

INDEX

CPSIA information can be obtained
at www.ICGtesting.com
Printed in the USA
LVHW080950130221
679240LV00009B/93